THIS WORKBOOK BELONGS TO:

_____

STUDENT WORKBOOK
TO KILL A MOCKINGBIRD

Use this workbook to get the most out of your reading.
Answer questions completely and thoughtfully.

COPYRIGHT INFORMATION

This is copyrighted material.

The purchaser may copy the student materials
for his or her classroom use only.
It may not be copied or distributed for any other purpose
without written permission from the publisher.

No portion may be posted on the Internet
without written permission from the publisher.

Copyright violations are prosecuted to the fullest extent of the law
and are subject to a minimum of a $500.00 fine,
imposed by the publisher
in addition to any other legal judgments obtained.

ISBN 978-1-60249-501-2
Copyright 2014
All Rights Reserved

Table Of Contents

Chapters 1-3
    Reading Activity 1: True or False 7
    Reading Activity 2: Analyzing Passages 10
    Reading Activity 3: Main and Minor Characters 13
    Reading Activity 4: Action, Character, Decision 14
    Reading Activity 5: Figurative Language 16
    Reading Activity 6: Elements of Fiction & Literary Devices 18
    Reading Activity 7: Meaning And Inferences 20
    Writing Activity 1: Who Are The Radleys? 24
    Suggested Writing Assignments 28
    Quick-Write Assignments 29

Chapters 4-7
    Reading Activity 1: True or False 33
    Reading Activity 2: Analyzing Passages 36
    Reading Activity 3: Static and Dynamic Characters 39
    Reading Activity 4: Action, Character, Decision 40
    Reading Activity 5: Figurative Language 41
    Reading Activity 6: Elements of Fiction & Literary Devices 43
    Reading Activity 7: Meaning And Inferences 45
    Writing Activity 1: How Is Jem And Scout's Relationship Changing? 47
    Suggested Writing Assignments 49
    Quick-Write Assignments 50

Chapters 8-11
    Reading Activity 1: True or False 53
    Reading Activity 2: Analyzing Passages 56
    Reading Activity 3: Static and Dynamic Characters 59
    Reading Activity 4: Action, Character, Decision 60
    Reading Activity 5: Figurative Language 61
    Reading Activity 6: Elements of Fiction & Literary Devices 63
    Reading Activity 7: Meaning And Inferences 64
    Writing Activity 1: How Are Characters Prejudiced? 66
    Suggested Writing Assignments 68
    Quick-Write Assignments 69

Chapters 12-14
    Reading Activity 1: True or False 73
    Reading Activity 2: Analyzing Passages 76
    Reading Activity 3: Characters Who Are Foils 79
    Reading Activity 4: Action, Character, Decision 80
    Reading Activity 5: Figurative Language 81
    Reading Activity 6: Elements of Fiction & Literary Devices 82
    Reading Activity 7: Meaning And Inferences 84
    Writing Activity 1: Who Is Calpurnia? 86
    Suggested Writing Assignments 88
    Quick-Write Assignments 89

Table Of Contents, Continued

Chapters 15-21
- Reading Activity 1: True or False   93
- Reading Activity 2: Analyzing Passages   96
- Reading Activity 3: Direct and Indirect Characterization   99
- Reading Activity 4: Action, Character, Decision   100
- Reading Activity 5: Figurative Language   101
- Reading Activity 6: Elements of Fiction & Literary Devices   102
- Reading Activity 7: Meaning And Inferences   103
- Writing Activity 1: What Is The Purpose Of The Trial?   106
- Suggested Writing Assignments   108
- Quick-Write Assignments   109

Chapters 22-31
- Reading Activity 1: True or False   113
- Reading Activity 2: Analyzing Passages   116
- Reading Activity 3: Round Character or Stereotype?   118
- Reading Activity 4: Action, Character, Decision   119
- Reading Activity 5: Figurative Language   120
- Reading Activity 6: Elements of Fiction & Literary Devices   122
- Reading Activity 7: Meaning And Inferences   123
- Writing Activity 1: How are Tom Robinson and Boo Radley alike?   125
- Suggested Writing Assignments   127
- Quick-Write Assignments   128

Overview
- Reading Activity 1: True or False   131
- Reading Activity 2: Analyzing Passages   134
- Reading Activity 3: Characters' Diction   137
- Reading Activity 4: Action, Character, Decision   138
- Reading Activity 5: Figurative Language   140
- Reading Activity 6: Elements of Fiction & Literary Devices   142
- Reading Activity 7: Meaning And Inferences   143
- Writing Activity 1: What role does fear play in To Kill A Mockingbird?   146
- Suggested Writing Assignments   149
- Quick-Write Assignments   150

MATERIALS: CHAPTERS 1-3
TO KILL A MOCKINGBIRD

Reading Activity 1: True or False

Reading Activity 2: Analyzing Passages

Reading Activity 3: Main and Minor Characters

Reading Activity 4: Action, Character, Decision

Reading Activity 5: Figurative Language

Reading Activity 6: Elements of Fiction & Literary Devices

Reading Activity 7: Meaning and Inferences

Writing Activity 1: Who Are The Radleys?

Suggested Writing Assignments

Quick-Write Assignments

Notes
To Kill A Mockingbird

To Kill A Mockingbird Chapters 1-3: True or False?

Write True or False in the blank next to each statement. Below the statement, explain why you chose true or false, referencing the text to support your choices.

_____ 1. Atticus won his first case and quickly became a rich lawyer.

_____ 2. The action of the story takes place during the Great Depression in the early 1930's.

_____ 3. The Radley Place brings the elements of Gothic fiction to the novel.

_____ 4. Most of the citizens of Maycomb are very religious.

_____ 5. Old Mr. Radley, Arthur "Boo" Radley's Father, loved his son.

To Kill A Mockingbird Chapters 1-3 True or False Worksheet Page 2

_____ 6. Jem gives Dill an accurate description of Boo Radley.

_____ 7. Calpurnia's relationship to Scout is more like a mother than like a nanny or housekeeper.

_____ 8. Miss Caroline has been well prepared for the challenges of managing her classroom.

_____ 9. Atticus believes that some circumstances require bending the law.

To Kill A Mockingbird Chapters 1-3 True or False Evaluation

List Your Group's Members: Your Group's Question # _____

_____ _____ _____ _____

1 = No, Not At All   **2** = A Little   **3** = Some   **4** = Yes   **5** = Yes, Very Well

Evaluation of Question # ___

Does the explanation support the answer of true or false?	1	2	3	4	5
Is there good textual evidence to support the answer?	1	2	3	4	5
Is the answer clearly stated?	1	2	3	4	5

Total Score _____ *of a possible 15 points*

Evaluation of Question # ___

Does the explanation support the answer of true or false?	1	2	3	4	5
Is there good textual evidence to support the answer?	1	2	3	4	5
Is the answer clearly stated?	1	2	3	4	5

Total Score _____ *of a possible 15 points*

Evaluation of Question # ___

Does the explanation support the answer of true or false?	1	2	3	4	5
Is there good textual evidence to support the answer?	1	2	3	4	5
Is the answer clearly stated?	1	2	3	4	5

Total Score _____ *of a possible 15 points*

Evaluation of Question # ___

Does the explanation support the answer of true or false?	1	2	3	4	5
Is there good textual evidence to support the answer?	1	2	3	4	5
Is the answer clearly stated?	1	2	3	4	5

Total Score _____ *of a possible 15 points*

To Kill A Mockingbird Chapters 1-3 Analyzing Passages

Answer the questions following the quotations completely.

1. "[Aunt Alexandra] married a man who spent most of his time lying in a hammock by the river wondering if his trot-lines were full." What does this tell you about Aunt Alexandra and her husband?

2. "Atticus's office in the courthouse contained little more than a hat rack, a spittoon, a checkerboard and an unsullied Code of Alabama." What can you infer from this statement?

3. In reference to Calpurnia, Scout says, "Our battles were epic and one-sided" and "I had felt her tyrannical presence as long as I could remember."

    a. What images do the words "epic battles" bring to mind?

    b. How is Harper Lee's word choice above more effective than simply saying, "We had a lot of big fights, and I always lost."

    c. What does the phrase "tyrannical presence" tell you about how Scout perceives the relationship between herself and Calpurnia?

To Kill A Mockingbird Chapters 1-3 Analyzing Passages Page 2

4. State what elements of the first meeting between Dill and the Finch children are humorous and explain why they are humorous.

5. Scout says about Boo Radley, "When people's azaleas froze in a cold snap, it was because he had breathed on them." What kind of an image of Boo Radley does this single sentence paint?

6. When Scout describes Maycomb, she uses words like "red slop" instead of "mud." She chooses to use the detail of bony mules in the "sweltering shade" flicking flies with their tails, and she says "the courthouse sagged in the square." The most memorable phrase is that ladies "were like soft teacakes with frostings of sweat and sweet talcum." Explain how each of these word choices affects our perception of the town of Maycomb.

7. In the last scene of Chapters 1-3, Dill dares Jem to touch the Radley house. What elements of this scene make it seem realistic, make it seem like something kids would really do?

8. The first chapter ends with "Flick. A tiny, almost invisible movement, and the house was still." What effect does this ending have?

To Kill A Mockingbird Chapters 1-3 Analyzing Passages Page 3

9. "I thought she was going to spit in it, which was the only reason anybody in Maycomb held out his hand: it was a time-honored method of sealing oral contracts. Wondering what bargain we had made, I turned to the class for an answer, but the class looked back at me in puzzlement. Miss Caroline picked up her ruler, gave me half a dozen quick little pats, then told me to stand in the corner. A storm of laughter broke loose when it finally occurred to the class that Miss Caroline had whipped me." What words here suggest confusion? What mood does it create?

10. "By the time we reached our front steps Walter had forgotten he was a Cunningham. Jem ran to the kitchen and asked Calpurnia to set an extra plate, we had company. Atticus greeted Walter and began a discussion about crops neither Jem nor I could follow."
In this passage, Walter is identified as "a Cunningham," as "company," and then as capable of having an "adult" conversation with Atticus. How does this relate to the idea of identity?

11. Little Chuck Little was another member of the population who didn't know where his next meal was coming from, but he was a born gentleman. Would the general population of Maycomb agree with the narrator's judgment of Little Chuck Little?

12. "First of all," he said, "if you can learn a simple trick, Scout, you'll get along a lot better with all kinds of folks. You never really understand a person until you consider things from his point of view...until you climb into his skin and walk around in it." What is Atticus asking Scout to do?

To Kill A Mockingbird Chapters 1-3 Main and Minor Characters

On the blank to the left of the name, write Main or Minor to identify the character as a main or minor character in the book. On the lines provided to the right of the characters' names, explain why you chose to identify each character as either main or minor, using evidence from the text. Go back and skim the text if you need to, to refresh your memory about these characters.

_____ Scout _____
_____

_____ Boo Radley _____
_____

_____ Calpurnia _____
_____

_____ Nathan Radley _____
_____

_____ Atticus _____
_____

_____ Jem _____
_____

_____ Miss Caroline _____
_____

_____ Mrs. Dubose _____
_____

_____ Dill _____
_____

_____ Miss Stephanie _____
_____

_____ Old Mr. Radley _____
_____

_____ Walter Cunningham _____
_____

_____ Burris Ewell _____
_____

To Kill A Mockingbird Chapters 1-3: Action, Character, Decision

Write A (for Action) C (for Character) or D (for Decision) in the blank next to each to identify whether the passage/statement advances the action, tells us more about a character, or provokes a decision. On the lines under each question, provide a short explanation of your choice.

___ 1. During his first five years in Maycomb, Atticus practiced economy more than anything; for several years thereafter he invested his earnings in his brother's education.

_____
_____
_____

___ 2. Dill had seen Dracula, a revelation that moved Jem to eye him with the beginning of respect.

_____
_____
_____

___ 3. But by the end of August our repertoire was vapid from countless reproductions, and it was then that Dill gave us the idea of making Boo Radley come out.

_____
_____
_____

___ 4. ...Dill made a mild concession: "I won't say you ran out on a dare an' I'll swap you The Gray Ghost if you just go up and touch the house."

_____
_____
_____

___ 5. Jem threw open the gate and sped to the side of the house, slapped it with his palm and ran back past us, not waiting to see if his foray was successful. Dill and I followed on his heels. Safely on our porch, panting and out of breath, we looked back.

_____
_____
_____

To Kill A Mockingbird Chapters 1-3: Action, Character, Decision Page 2

___ 6. Walter Cunningham's face told everybody in the first grade he had hookworms. His absence of shoes told us how he got them.

_____
_____
_____

___ 7. Jem suddenly grinned at him. "Come on home to dinner with us, Walter," he said. "We'd be glad to have you."

_____
_____
_____

___ 8. "It's alive!" she screamed.

_____
_____
_____

___ 9. "Don't know how. They call me Burris't home."

_____
_____
_____

To Kill A Mockingbird Chapters 1-3: Figurative Language

On the short line provided, write P for personification or S for simile. On the lines under each question, explain what the figurative language means.

____ 1. Maycomb...was a tired old town.
_____
_____

____ 2. The courthouse sagged in the square.
_____
_____

____ 3. ...[ladies] were like soft teacakes with frostings of sweat and sweet talcum
_____
_____

____ 4. The remains of a picket drunkenly guarded the front yard.
_____
_____

____ 5. ...from the Radley chicken yard tall pecan trees shook their fruit into the schoolyard.
_____
_____

____ 6. {Dill's} hair was snow white and stuck to his head like duckfluff.
_____
_____

____ 7. My memory came alive to see Mrs. Radley occasionally open the front door...and pour water on her cannas.
_____
_____

____ 8. ...the Radley Place drew [Dill] as the moon draws water.
_____
_____

____ 9. The old house was the same, droopy and sick.
_____
_____

____ 10. ...watching the gate hanging crazily on its homemade hinge
_____
_____

To Kill A Mockingbird Chapters 1-3: Figurative Language Page 2

___ 11. Walter looked as if he had been raised on fish food: his eyes, as blue as Dill Harris's, were red-rimmed and watery.
_____
_____

___ 12. When I passed the Radley Place for the fourth time that day — twice at a full gallop — my gloom had deepened to match the house.
_____
_____

___ 13. They were people, but they lived like animals.
_____
_____

To Kill A Mockingbird Chapters 1-3: Elements of Fiction & Literary Devices

1. Look at the dialogue among the children when Dill emerges from the collard patch, and evaluate it. Is it realistic? What makes it realistic? Is it humorous? Why or why not?

   _____
   _____
   _____

2. Where else in the first chapter do we see examples of humor?

   _____
   _____
   _____

3. It is mentioned that "the sheriff hadn't the heart to put [Boo] in jail alongside Negroes." What theme in the book does this statement introduce or foreshadow?

   _____
   _____
   _____

4. The courthouse is mentioned several times in the first chapter, foreshadowing that it will play an important role in the story. List 3 things that happen(ed) at the courthouse in Chapters 1-3.

   _____
   _____
   _____

5. What theme does the dialogue about the turtle introduce? Of what could the image of the turtle be symbolic?

   _____
   _____
   _____

6. What elements in Chapters 1-3 are stereotypes?

   _____
   _____
   _____

7. What elements does Harper Lee use to build suspense in Chapters 1-3?

   _____
   _____
   _____

To Kill A Mockingbird Chapters 1-3: Elements of Fiction & Literary Devices Page 2

8. What is Scout's main conflict?
   _____
   _____
   _____

9. Note the mentions of the Radley house in these chapters. What words are used to describe it? What mood does this create?
   _____
   _____
   _____

10. One of the major themes in the novel is growing up. List three examples from these chapters that exemplify that theme.
    _____
    _____
    _____

To Kill A Mockingbird Chapters 1-3: Meaning & Inferences 1

Read the passages and answer the related questions.

1. When enough years had gone by to enable us to look back on them, we sometimes discussed the events leading to his accident. What does this sentence tell us about the narrator of the story and the time that the story takes place?

   _____
   _____
   _____

2. We were far too old to settle an argument with a fist-fight, so we consulted Atticus. Our father said we were both right. Who is Atticus?

   _____
   _____
   _____

3. … [Alexandra] married a taciturn man who spent most of his time lying in a hammock by the river wondering if his trot-lines were full. What words could you use to accurately describe Alexandra's husband?

   _____
   _____
   _____

4. Atticus's office in the courthouse contained little more than a hat rack, a spittoon, a checkerboard and an unsullied Code of Alabama. What does this description tell you about Atticus's law practice at this time?

   _____
   _____
   _____

5. He played with us, read to us, and treated us with courteous detachment. Based on the facts given in this sentence, describe the relationship between Atticus Finch and his children.

   _____
   _____
   _____

To Kill A Mockingbird Chapters 1-3: Meaning & Inferences 1 Page 2

6. "Miss Caroline seemed unaware that the ragged, denim-shirted and floursack-skirted first grade, most of whom had chopped cotton and fed hogs from the time they were able to walk, were immune to imaginative literature." What does "immune" imply in this passage?

___

7. "I mumbled that I was sorry and retired meditating upon my crime. I never deliberately learned to read, but somehow I had been wallowing illicitly in the daily papers." What do the words "crime" and "illicitly" suggest about how the narrator views the situation?

___

8. "He ain't company, Cal, he's just a Cunningham-" What does this reveal about Scout's view of society in Maycomb?

___

To Kill A Mockingbird Chapters 1-3: Meaning & Inferences 2

Read the passages and answer the related questions.

1. I asked Dill where his father was...

    "I haven't got one."

    "Is he dead?"

    "No..."

    "Then if he's not dead you've got one, haven't you?"

    Dill blushed and Jem told me to hush....

    Why does Dill blush and why does Jem tell Scout to hush?

    _____
    _____
    _____

2. Jem figured Mr. Radley kept [Boo] chained to the bed most of the time. Atticus said no, it wasn't that sort of thing, that there were other ways of making people into ghosts. What does Atticus mean?

    _____
    _____
    _____

3. What things in Chapters 1-3 are facts? Which things are opinions?

Facts:
_____
_____
_____
_____
_____

Opinions:
_____
_____
_____
_____
_____
_____

To Kill A Mockingbird Chapters 1-3: Meaning & Inferences 3

"Don't worry, Scout," Jem comforted me. "Our teacher says Miss Caroline's introducing a new way of teaching. She learned about it in college. It'll be in all the grades soon. You don't have to learn much out of books that way — it's like if you wanta learn about cows, you go milk one, see?"
"Yeah Jem, but I don't wanta study cows, I-"

"Sure you do. You hafta know about cows, they're a big part of life in Maycomb County."

I contented myself with asking Jem if he'd lost his mind.

"'I'm just trying to tell you the new way they're teachin' the first grade, stubborn. It's the Dewey Decimal System.'

Having never questioned Jem's pronouncements, I saw no reason to begin now. The Dewey Decimal System consisted, in part, of Miss Caroline waving cards at us on which were printed 'the,' 'cat,' 'rat,' 'man,' and 'you.' No comment seemed to be expected of us, and the class received these impressionistic revelations in silence. I was bored, so I began a letter to Dill. Miss Caroline caught me writing and told me to tell my father to stop teaching me. 'Besides,' she said. 'We don't write in the first grade, we print. You won't learn to write until you're in the third grade.'"

Note: Jem is a little confused. The Dewey Decimal System is a system used to classify library books. A philosopher named John Dewey studied the best ways to educate children, which is what Miss Caroline would have learned about at college.

1. Describe Miss Caroline's new method of teaching.

2. The line "I contented myself…" could be written as dialogue, but instead it is written from the narrator's perspective. What is the effect of that difference?

3. What does "impressionistic revelations" mean?

4. Why is Miss Caroline's request for Scout to stop writing her letter ironic?

To Kill A Mockingbird Chapters 1-3: Who Are The Radleys?

There is a lot of information about the Radleys in this first chapter. Who are the Radleys, really?

When we read information, we have to consider the source to determine if what we are reading is likely to be true or not. We have to try to determine whether or not we should believe what is being said and whether or not we agree with it. This is called critical reading, an essential skill to develop in our Information Age, as it is called.

There is so much information online, on television, and from other sources; we need to consider the information we get with a critical eye to determine what is fact from opinion, what is true from what is false, and what spin might be being put onto facts because of the background or motives of the person or people who put out the information.

Using the information given in Chapters 1-3 to determine who the Radleys really are is more than an exercise in character study; it is an exercise to demonstrate and practice essential critical reading skills. Remember the process by which you study the Radleys, and practice using that critical reading, critical thinking process with other information you encounter.

To determine who the Radleys are you need to:
1. Gather the information given about the Radleys
2. Determine the source(s) of that information
3. Determine whether the source(s) are each reliable or not by considering
    a. whether they have first-hand knowledge or not
    b. whether they have any prejudices or biases
    c. whether they have any ulterior motives in presenting the facts in a particular way
    d. whether they are capable of delivering true information

4. Determine which statements are likely to be facts, which are likely to be opinions, and which may be tainted by background, biases, ulterior motives, or other characteristics of the source
5. Consider the facts in the light of your own personal knowledge and other factors
6. Decide with which statements you agree or disagree
7. Come to your own conclusion as to what you believe

To Kill A Mockingbird Chapters 1-3: Who Are The Radleys?

Complete as many of these charts as you need to analyze all the information about the Radleys given in Chapters 1-3.

Textual Information (It helps to include page number)	Source	First-Hand?	Fact or Opinion?	Reliable?	What You Think

To Kill A Mockingbird Chapters 1-3: Who Are The Radleys?

After you complete analyzing the textual information about the Radleys, compare the Radleys to others in the town on the criteria given in the middle column:

Townspeople	Point of Comparison	Radleys
	Are they religious?	
	Are they social?	
	Do they have money?	
	Do they try to do what they think is the right thing?	
	How do people treat them?	

Use Your Own Knowledge

1. If you were the Radleys how would you feel about the townspeople?

2. When you were a kid, was there anyone or any place you were afraid of, and now that you are older do you look at that person or place differently?

3. Are things and people always the way they seem to be?

To Kill A Mockingbird Chapters 1-3: Who Are The Radleys?

You have looked at the textual evidence and evaluated it. You have looked at the Radleys in comparison to the townspeople. You have considered some applicable points from your own experience. Taking all of these things into consideration, write a composition in which you answer the question, "Who are the Radleys?".

Write your rough drafts on your own paper and then copy your final, best composition onto this page, or submit a printed-out copy.

To Kill A Mockingbird Chapters 1-3: Writing Assignments

1. Write a letter from Mrs. Radley to Nathan asking him to come and stay with her and Arthur after his father's funeral. Consider her situation and use all valid points you think she would make.

2. Make up a story that could have been one of the legends about the Radley Place that Jem could have told Scout and Dill.

3. Write a poem describing Maycomb.

4. Scout gives a good account of her family's history. Write an account of your own family's history trying to make it as interesting and fun to read as Scout's is.

5. Choose one of your relatives who has had an interesting life and write his or her story.

6. From Scout's description, we can picture Maycomb in our mind's eye. Write a description of your town (or any town you know well) using interesting imagery and figurative language, as Scout does, to bring your town to life.

7. Write Mr. Radley's obituary notice.

8. Create the dialogue for the conversation between Mr. Radley and Boo after Boo stabbed Mr. Radley's leg with the scissors.

9. Make a list of the main events in Chapters 1-3 in the order in which they actually happen in chronological time.

10. Make an outline of points you would have used (including supporting points) to persuade Mr. Radley to either send Boo to the industrial school with the other boys or to send Boo to Tuscaloosa for some psychological counseling.

11. You are Boo Radley. Write a journal entry for the day you came home in your father's custody (instead of being sent with the other boys to the industrial school). Continue to write journal entries as Boo Radley for each day that we study this novel.

12. Describe the relationship between Jem and Scout, beyond the mere fact that they are brother and sister.

13. Write the letter that Scout was writing to Dill.

14. Write a paragraph from Miss Caroline's perspective about how the first day of school went.

15. Write a description of Walter Cunningham's day, beginning with farm work and ending with school.

16. Explain why Scout went from being excited about starting school to dreading it.

17. Describe how the students make up a microcosm of Maycomb.

To Kill A Mockingbird Chapters 1-3: Quick-Write Writing Assignments

1. You are Jem. What do you think of Dill?

2. You are Arthur "Boo" Radley. What do you think of Jem's running up to touch your house and running away again?

3. You are Atticus. What do you think about your own children?

4. What would have persuaded you to run up and touch the Radley house?

5. Describe Maycomb.

6. Why does Dill want to make Boo Radley come out?

7. Choose three words to describe Scout and explain why you chose those particular words.

8. Compare the adventure stories Jem and Dill liked to read with something related to adventure that boys like today.

9. What do you think of Scout? Do you think she'd be a fun friend?

10. What is your favorite image, phrase, or scene in Chapters 1-3? Why?

11. How did Scout behave badly during lunch?

12. In what ways were characters humiliated in these chapters?

13. Is Miss Caroline a good teacher?

14. Why does Atticus think bending the law is justified?

15. What is a compromise? Is the one Atticus makes moral?

MATERIALS: CHAPTERS 4-7
TO KILL A MOCKINGBIRD

Reading Activity 1: True or False

Reading Activity 2: Analyzing Passages

Reading Activity 3: Static and Dynamic Characters

Reading Activity 4: Action, Character, Decision

Reading Activity 5: Figurative Language

Reading Activity 6: Elements of Fiction & Literary Devices

Reading Activity 7: Meaning and Inferences

Writing Activity 1: How Is Jem and Scout's Relationship Changing?

Suggested Writing Assignments

Quick-Write Assignments

Notes
To Kill A Mockingbird

To Kill a Mockingbird Chapters 4-7: True or False?

Write *True* or *False* in the blank next to each statement. Below the statement, explain why you chose true or false, referencing the text to support your choices.

_____ 1. The primary adults in Scout's life view Boo Radley with judgment and lack of compassion.

_____ 2. The escalation of the children's fascination with Boo Radley is becoming dangerous.

_____ 3. Scout is increasingly unable to understand Jem's reactions to situations.

_____ 4. Jem, Scout and Dill find lying to be an immoral behavior they avoid.

To Kill a Mockingbird Chapters 4-7: True or False Worksheet Page 2

_____ 5. Jem believes that the oak tree on the Radley property is dying.

_____ 6. Dill is a negative influence on Jem and Scout.

To Kill a Mockingbird Chapters 4-7 True or False Evaluation

List Your Group's Members: Your Group's Question # _____

_____   _____   _____

_____   _____   _____

1 = No, Not At All   **2** = A Little   **3** = Some   **4** = Yes   **5** = Yes, Very Well

Evaluation of Question # ___
Does the explanation support the answer of true or false?   1   2   3   4   5
Is there good textual evidence to support the answer?   1   2   3   4   5
Is the answer clearly stated?   1   2   3   4   5
                            Total Score _____ of a possible 15 points

Evaluation of Question # ___
Does the explanation support the answer of true or false?   1   2   3   4   5
Is there good textual evidence to support the answer?   1   2   3   4   5
Is the answer clearly stated?   1   2   3   4   5
                            Total Score _____ of a possible 15 points

Evaluation of Question # ___
Does the explanation support the answer of true or false?   1   2   3   4   5
Is there good textual evidence to support the answer?   1   2   3   4   5
Is the answer clearly stated?   1   2   3   4   5
                            Total Score _____ of a possible 15 points

Evaluation of Question # ___
Does the explanation support the answer of true or false?   1   2   3   4   5
Is there good textual evidence to support the answer?   1   2   3   4   5
Is the answer clearly stated?   1   2   3   4   5
                            Total Score _____ of a possible 15 points

Evaluation of Question # ___
Does the explanation support the answer of true or false?   1   2   3   4   5
Is there good textual evidence to support the answer?   1   2   3   4   5
Is the answer clearly stated?   1   2   3   4   5
                            Total Score _____ of a possible 15 points

To Kill a Mockingbird Chapters 4-7 Analyzing Passages

Answer the questions following the quotations completely.

1. "Well, Indian-heads—well, they come from the Indians. They're real strong magic, they make you have good luck. Not like fried chicken when you're not lookin' for it, but things like long life 'n' good health, 'n' passin' six-weeks tests… these are real valuable to somebody. I'm gonna put 'em in my trunk." Before Jem went to his room, he looked for a long time at the Radley Place. He seemed to be thinking again. What is revealed about Jem as he describes his feelings about treasures found in the knothole? What do his observations show readers about his maturity level?

2. "Jem was a born hero." Locate this passage in chapter 4 of your book. Scout (as the narrator) makes this observation about her brother. Does it make a difference to the meaning if a reader assumes that the "grown up" Scout thinks this? Based on the surrounding text, do you think that young Scout felt this way about her brother? Why or why not?

3. "We weren't makin' fun of him, we weren't laughin' at him," said Jem, "we were just-"
"So that was what you were doing, wasn't it?"
"Makin' fun of him?"
"No," said Atticus, "putting his life's history on display for the edification of the neighborhood."
Jem seemed to swell a little. "I didn't say we were doin' that, I didn't say it!"
Atticus grinned dryly. "You just told me," he said. "You stop this nonsense right now, every one of you."

Just after this passage, Atticus mentions that Jem has said that he wanted to be a lawyer when he grew up. Since lawyers both interpret laws/situations and argue for them, what is Jem's objective here? Of what is he attempting to convince Atticus? Is he successful?

To Kill a Mockingbird Chapters 4-7: Analyzing Passages Page 2

4. Miss Maudie settled her bridgework. "You know old Mr. Radley was a foot-washing Baptist-"
"That's what you are, ain't it?"
"My shell's not that hard, child. I'm just a Baptist."
"Don't you all believe in foot-washing?"
"We do. At home in the bathtub."
"But we can't have communion with you all-"
Apparently deciding that it was easier to define primitive baptistry than closed communion, Miss Maudie said: "Foot-washers believe anything that's pleasure is a sin. Did you know some of 'em came out of the woods one Saturday and passed by this place and told me me and my flowers were going to hell?"

In this passage, Miss Maudie is trying to explain an important nuanced difference to Scout. What are all the different distinctions made in this passage? What does the passage show about Scout's worldview?

5. "Gracious child, I was raveling a thread, wasn't even thinking about your father, but now that I am I'll say this: Atticus Finch is the same in his house as he is on the public streets."
What are the difference connotations associated with "house" and "streets"? What do these differences reveal about Atticus's character? How does it relate to Atticus's profession?

To Kill a Mockingbird Chapters 4-7: Analyzing Passages Page 3

6. It was then, I suppose, that Jem and I first began to part company. Sometimes I did not understand him, but my periods of bewilderment were short-lived. This was beyond me. "Please," I pleaded, "can'tcha just think about it for a minute—by yourself on that place—" Why is the phrase "I suppose" significant here? How would the meaning change if it were removed?

7. "As Atticus once advised me to do, I tried to climb into Jem's skin and walk around in it: if I had gone alone to the Radley Place at two in the morning, my funeral would have been held the next afternoon." What is Atticus actually asking Scout to do? Based on the passage, is she successful at this challenge (hint: consider the phrase after the colon)?

8. Consider Scout's observations of Jem after the knothole is sealed: "He stood there until nightfall, and I waited for him. When we went in the house I saw he had been crying; his face was dirty in the right places, but I thought it odd that I had not heard him." Consider the use of the word "odd." What significance does that word have in the passage? What does it show about the changing relationship between brother and sister?

To Kill a Mockingbird Chapters 4-7
Reading Activity 3: Static and Dynamic Characters

A character can be either dynamic or static. A dynamic character grows or progresses in some way as plot in a story moves forward. A static character does not undergo a change and stays fundamentally the same.

From the list of characters below, put the names of dynamic characters in the relevant boxes and names of static characters in the relevant boxes. Complete the chart, using actual quotes when asked and noting page numbers. Go back and skim the text if you need to, to refresh your memory about these characters.

Scout | Boo Radley | Miss Maudie | Nathan Radley | Atticus | Jem | Dill

Name of Dynamic Character	Quote – Observation 1 (Find a quote that shows how a character was before changing. Write the quote below.)	Quote – Observation 2 (Find a quote that shows how a character has undergone change. Write the quote below.)	Describe the Character's Change

Name of Static Character	Quote – Observation 1 (Find a quote that describes a quality or attitude of a static character. Write the quote below.)	Quote – Observation 2 (Find a quote later in the novel that shows that the character has the same quality or attitude. Write the quote below.)	Describe the Character's Quality or Attitude

To Kill a Mockingbird Chapters 4-7: Action, Character, Decision

Write **A** (for Action) **C** (for Character) or **D** (for Decision) in the blank next to each to identify whether the passage/statement advances the action, tells us more about a character, or provokes a decision. On the lines under each question, provide a short explanation of your choice.

___ 1. For some reason, my first year of school had wrought a great change in our relationship: Calpurnia's tyranny, unfairness, and meddling in my business had faded to gentle grumblings of general disapproval. On my part, I went to much trouble, sometimes, not to provoke her.

___ 2. Finders were keepers unless title was proven. Plucking an occasional camellia, getting a squirt of hot milk from Miss Maudie Atkinson's cow on a summer day, helping ourselves to someone's scuppernongs was part of our ethical culture, but money was different.

___ 3. Miss Maudie hated her house: time spent indoors was time wasted.

___ 4. There he was, returning to me. His white shirt bobbed over the back fence and slowly grew larger. He came up the back steps, latched the door behind him, and sat on his cot. Wordlessly, he held up his pants. He lay down, and for a while I heard his cot trembling. Soon he was still. I did not hear him stir again.

___ 5. Someone had filled our knot-hole with cement.

To Kill a Mockingbird Chapters 4-7: Figurative Language

On the short line provided, write **H** for hyperbole or **I** for irony. On the lines under each question, explain how the figurative language helps create meaning.

___ 1. Jem stamped his foot. "Don't you know you're not supposed to even touch the trees over there? You'll get killed if you do!"

___ 2. Mrs. Dubose lived two doors up the street from us; neighborhood opinion was unanimous that Mrs. Dubose was the meanest old woman who ever lived.

___ 3. I was fairly sure Boo Radley was inside that house, but I couldn't prove it, and felt it best to keep my mouth shut or I would be accused of believing in Hot Steams, phenomena I was immune to in the daytime.

___ 4. Through all the head-shaking, quelling of nausea and Jem-yelling, I had heard another sound, so low I could not have heard it from the sidewalk. Someone inside the house was laughing.

___ 5. When I admired them and hoped I would have some eventually, she said, "Look here." With a click of her tongue she thrust out her bridgework, a gesture of cordiality that cemented our friendship.

___ 6. "Well how'd you feel if you'd been shut up for a hundred years with nothin' but cats to eat? I bet he's got a beard down to here-"...

___ 7. Jem said, "Okay." When I protested, he said sweetly, "You don't have to come along, Angel May."

___ 8. Atticus saved Dill from immediate dismemberment. "Just a minute, Miss Rachel," he said. "I've never heard of 'em doing that before. Were you all playing cards?" Jem fielded Dill's fly with his eyes shut: "No sir, just with matches."

To Kill a Mockingbird Chapters 4-7: Figurative Language Page 2

___ 9. He was struggling into his shirt. "I've got to."
"You do an' I'll wake up Atticus."
"You do and I'll kill you."

_____
_____

___ 10. Less than two weeks later we found a whole package of chewing gum, which we enjoyed, the fact that everything on the Radley Place was poison having slipped Jem's memory.

_____
_____

To Kill a Mockingbird Chapters 4-7: Elements of Fiction & Literary Devices

1. One of the motifs in the novel is seasons, especially summer. Consider this passage:

   Summer was on the way; Jem and I awaited it with impatience. Summer was our best season: it was sleeping on the back screened porch in cots, or trying to sleep in the treehouse; summer was everything good to eat; it was a thousand colors in a parched landscape; but most of all, summer was Dill.

   What do the different examples have in common? What does this show about how Jem and Scout view summer? Why do they value it?

2. What does the knothole symbolize?

3. A major theme in the novel is the relationship between good and evil. List ways that good and evil are confused, reversed or unclear in chapters 4-7.

4. Imagery of the moon recurs to create a motif in the novel. Consider this passage:

   [Jem] pointed to the east. A gigantic moon was rising behind Miss Maudie's pecan trees. "That makes it seem hotter," he said.
   "Cross in it tonight?" asked Dill, not looking up. He was constructing a cigarette from newspaper and string.
   "No, just the lady. Don't light that thing, Dill, you'll stink up this whole end of town."
   There was a lady in the moon in Maycomb. She sat at a dresser combing her hair.

   What are the children observing about the moon? Why might a "cross" or a "lady" be significant? How are their observations related to the idea of imagination?

To Kill a Mockingbird Chapters 4-7: Elements of Fiction & Literary Devices Page 2

5. Consider the gifts that Jem and Scout received: gum, pennies, twine, soap dolls, spelling bee medal, pocket watch and knife. Do these objects have any qualities in common? Are they suitable gifts for Jem and Scout? What is the significance of them?

6. A major theme in the novel is prejudice. List examples of ways that characters have made judgments about each other, which may or may not be true.

To Kill a Mockingbird Chapters 4-7: Meaning & Inferences 1

Read the passages and answer the related questions.

1. *Jem's head at times was transparent: he had thought that up to make me understand he wasn't afraid of Radleys in any shape or form, to contrast his own fearless heroism with my cowardice.*

What does this sentence tell us about the relationship between Scout and Jem?

2. *"Thing is, foot-washers think women are a sin by definition. They take the Bible literally, you know."*

What does Miss Maudie mean when she makes this claim?

3. *We eased in beside Miss Maudie, who looked around. "Where were you all, didn't you hear the commotion?"*
   "What happened?" asked Jem.
   "Mr. Radley shot at a Negro in his collard patch."
   "Oh. Did he hit him?"
   "No," said Miss Stephanie. "Shot in the air. Scared him pale, though. Says if anybody sees a white nigger around, that's the one. Says he's got the other barrel waitin' for the next sound he hears in that patch, an' next time he won't aim high, be it dog, nigger, or—Jem Finch!"

Since the reader already knows that the children caused the disturbance which prompted Nathan Radley to fire his gun, what is the point of including this story? What does it show about Nathan Radley, who made it up, or about Miss Stephanie, who repeats it?

4. *[Jem] declared Egyptians walked that way; I said if they did I didn't see how they got anything done, but Jem said they accomplished more than the Americans ever did, they invented toilet paper and perpetual embalming, and asked where would we be today if they hadn't? Atticus told me to delete the adjectives and I'd have the facts."*

What advice is Atticus giving Scout? What is he advising her to do?

5. *"Well maybe it is. I'm sure Mr. Radley knows more about his trees than we do."*

Why does Atticus contradict his earlier opinion here? What message is he sending to Jem?

To Kill a Mockingbird Chapters 4-7: Meaning & Inferences 2

Read the passage and answer the related questions.

Jem waved my words away as if fanning gnats. He was silent for a while, then he said, "When I went back for my breeches—they were all in a tangle when I was gettin' out of 'em, I couldn't get 'em loose. When I went back—" Jem took a deep breath. "When I went back, they were folded across the fence... like they were expectin' me."
"Across—"
"And something else—" Jem's voice was flat. "Show you when we get home.
They'd been sewed up. Not like a lady sewed 'em, like somethin' I'd try to do.
All crooked. It's almost like—"
"—somebody knew you were comin' back for 'em."
Jem shuddered. "Like somebody was readin' my mind... like somebody could tell what I was gonna do. Can't anybody tell what I'm gonna do lest they know me, can they, Scout?"
Jem's question was an appeal. I reassured him: "Can't anybody tell what you're gonna do lest they live in the house with you, and even I can't tell sometimes."

1. What does Jem find so troubling about his experience?

2. Why is it interesting that Scout finishes Jem's sentence?

3. Given the structure of the book and the way it unfolds the sequence of events, why is this conversation significant? How might it relate to the reader?

To Kill a Mockingbird Chapters 4-7:
How is Jem and Scout's relationship changing?

In chapters 4-7, as the plot advances and the children become more fascinated by the reclusive Boo Radley, the dynamic in the relationship between Jem and Scout is changing. At multiple points, Jem actively excludes Scout from playing and criticizes her ability to relate to him because she is a girl. Scout has moments when she understand her brother's motivations perfectly and others when she cannot understand why he reacts emotionally in certain situations.

Often when siblings communicate, the words they say to each other only convey some of the meaning. Sometimes the way it is said or the context it is said in creates additional meaning. This can often be observed when siblings have opposing ideas. Looking closely at the text for this deeper, additional meaning is called *critical reading,* a key skill for accomplished readers.

Using textual evidence from chapters 4-7, look for patterns to begin formulating an answer to the question "How is Jem and Scout's relationship changing?". As you develop an answer, consider why it is significant. What does this shift reveal about the characters? How does it create meaning in the book?

To determine an idea about Jem and Scout's relationship:

1. Identify passages and quotes where Jem and Scout interact.

2. Examine the context of your quotes.

3. Consider the connotation and denotation of key phrases in your quotes.

    a. What is the tone—friendly, adversarial, angry, concerned?
    b. What is the main conflict between the siblings ?
    c. What are the characters revealing or concealing in their language?

4. Look for patterns in your evidence. Is a word or idea repeated? Use these patterns to shape an answer to the question.

To Kill a Mockingbird Chapters 4-7:
How is Jem and Scout's relationship changing?

Use this chart (and additional pages, if needed) to collect, analyze and evaluate information about Jem and Scout's relationship.

Quote (and page number)	Paraphrase Quote	What is the deeper meaning implied in quote?	How/why does quote show change is occurring?	Why is this significant? What does it reveal about the relationship?

To Kill a Mockingbird Chapters 4-7:
Creative Analytical Writing Assignments

1. Write a letter from Dill to his mother telling her about his friends Jem and Scout and the fun games they spend summer days playing.

2. Make up a story that could have been one of the legends about the Radley Place that Jem could have told Scout and Dill.

3. In the format of a play, write dialogue from one of the children's "Boo Radley" games. Include details mentioned in the text (example: Mrs. Radley's missing right forefinger, Boo whittling all the family's furniture, etc.).

4. Write a brief description of what Boo saw Scout doing through the window that made him laugh.

5. Pretend you are Scout's teacher. Write a note on her report card that describes her behavior in school.

6. Write your own version of the letter from Jem and Scout to their mysterious gift-giver.

7. Find a passage in these chapters where "grown up" Scout is narrating. Rewrite the passage, imagining that you are "grown up" Jem.

8. Make a list of the ways that the novel is a mystery story and explain why the elements create suspense.

9. Imagine that Boo keeps a diary. Write a diary entry about the decision to leave gifts for Jem and Scout. Include details about why you feel motivated to give and what you hope the recipients will think and feel.

10. Write an essay called "What I did over summer vacation" from Jem's perspective.

11. Write a children's picture book about the importance of being "the same in the house as [one] is on the public streets."

12. Just like Scout imagines what it might be like to walk around in Jem's skin, select another character from the novel and write about what it might be like to walk around in his or her skin.

To Kill a Mockingbird Chapters 4-7: Quick-Write Writing Assignments

1. Despite Jem's protestations, is the "Boo Radley" game cruel?
2. Who is right, Scout or Jem, when it comes to deciding to retrieve Jem's pants?
3. Of all the trinket gifts, which one is the best? Why?
4. Does Jem behave like a hero?
5. Is Nathan Radley's response to the noise in his yard justified?
6. What clues suggest that Boo is the gift-giver? Why?
7. Compare "grown up" Scout narration to Scout's dialogue in the present day. Are the characters similar? Which Scout do you like better?
8. In chapters 4-7, Atticus often thinks like a lawyer as he parents. Is this a positive or negative?
9. Why is Miss Maudie so passionate about nut grass? Does it relate to any other themes or motifs?
10. Why does Jem cry at the end of chapter 7?

MATERIALS: CHAPTERS 8-11
TO KILL A MOCKINGBIRD

Reading Activity 1: True or False

Reading Activity 2: Analyzing Passages

Reading Activity 3: Static and Dynamic Characters

Reading Activity 4: Action, Character, Decision

Reading Activity 5: Figurative Language

Reading Activity 6: Elements of Fiction & Literary Devices

Reading Activity 7: Meaning and Inferences

Writing Activity 1: How Are Characters Prejudiced?

Suggested Writing Assignments

Quick-Write Assignments

Notes
To Kill A Mockingbird

To Kill A Mockingbird Chapters 8-11: True or False?

Write *True* or *False* in the blank next to each statement. Below the statement, explain why you chose true or false, referencing the text to support your choices.

_____ 1. Jem and Scout understand why community members criticize Atticus.

_____ 2. Atticus' family has very different values than Atticus.

_____ 3. Mrs. Dubose hates Jem and Scout.

_____ 4. Scout's behavior is out of control because she lacks strong parenting.

To Kill A Mockingbird Chapters 8-11 True or False Worksheet Page 2

_____ 5. Atticus is a weak man.

_____ 6. Scout and Jem have a clear understanding of their father's personality.

To Kill A Mockingbird Chapters 8-11 True or False Evaluation

List Your Group's Members: Your Group's Question # _____

_____ _____ _____

_____ _____ _____

1 = No, Not At All   **2** = A Little   **3** = Some   **4** = Yes   **5** = Yes, Very Well

Evaluation of Question # ___
Does the explanation support the answer of true or false?   1   2   3   4   5
Is there good textual evidence to support the answer?   1   2   3   4   5
Is the answer clearly stated?   1   2   3   4   5
Total Score _____ of a possible 15 points

Evaluation of Question # ___
Does the explanation support the answer of true or false?   1   2   3   4   5
Is there good textual evidence to support the answer?   1   2   3   4   5
Is the answer clearly stated?   1   2   3   4   5
Total Score _____ of a possible 15 points

Evaluation of Question # ___
Does the explanation support the answer of true or false?   1   2   3   4   5
Is there good textual evidence to support the answer?   1   2   3   4   5
Is the answer clearly stated?   1   2   3   4   5
Total Score _____ of a possible 15 points

Evaluation of Question # ___
Does the explanation support the answer of true or false?   1   2   3   4   5
Is there good textual evidence to support the answer?   1   2   3   4   5
Is the answer clearly stated?   1   2   3   4   5
Total Score _____ of a possible 15 points

Evaluation of Question # ___
Does the explanation support the answer of true or false?   1   2   3   4   5
Is there good textual evidence to support the answer?   1   2   3   4   5
Is the answer clearly stated?   1   2   3   4   5
Total Score _____ of a possible 15 points

To Kill A Mockingbird Chapters 8-11 Analyzing Passages

Answer the questions following the quotations completely.

1. "Atticus said, 'Whoa, son,' so gently that I was greatly heartened. It was obvious that he had not followed a word Jem said, for all Atticus said was, 'You're right. We'd better keep this and the blanket to ourselves. Someday, maybe, Scout can thank him for covering her up.'" Why is the word "obvious" ironic here? From what Atticus says, does he understand what Jem has conveyed to him?

2. "'If you shouldn't be defendin' him, then why are you doin' it?'
'For a number of reasons,' said Atticus. 'The main one is, if I didn't I couldn't hold up my head in town, I couldn't represent this county in the legislature, I couldn't even tell you or Jem not to do something again.' What does Atticus mean here? How are the ideas of fair representation or justice affecting him personally?

3. "Aunt Alexandra was fanatical on the subject of my attire. I could not possibly hope to be a lady if I wore breeches; when I said I could do nothing in a dress, she said I wasn't supposed to be doing things that required pants. Aunt Alexandra's vision of my deportment involved playing with small stoves, tea sets, and wearing the Add-A-Pearl necklace she gave me when I was born; furthermore, I should be a ray of sunshine in my father's lonely life. I suggested that one could be a ray of sunshine in pants just as well, but Aunty said that one had to behave like a sunbeam, that I was born good but had grown progressively worse every year." Contrast Aunt Alexandra's values with Scout's. How does Alexandra feel about her? About Atticus's parenting?

To Kill A Mockingbird Chapters 8-11 Analyzing Passages Page 2

4. "'Right. But do you think I could face my children otherwise? You know what's going to happen as well as I do, Jack, and I hope and pray I can get Jem and Scout through it without bitterness, and most of all, without catching Maycomb's usual disease. Why reasonable people go stark raving mad when anything involving a Negro comes up, is something I don't pretend to understand. . . I just hope that Jem and Scout come to me for their answers instead of listening to the town. I hope they trust me enough. . .'" What is the "usual disease"? What context clues help you to understand that?

5. "'When he gave us our air-rifles Atticus wouldn't teach us to shoot. Uncle Jack instructed us in the rudiments thereof; he said Atticus wasn't interested in guns. Atticus said to Jem one day, 'I'd rather you shot at tin cans in the back yard, but I know you'll go after birds. Shoot all the bluejays you want, if you can hit 'em, but remember it's a sin To Kill A Mockingbird.'

That was the only time I ever heard Atticus say it was a sin to do something, and I asked Miss Maudie about it.

'Your father's right," she said. "Mockingbirds don't do one thing but make music for us to enjoy. They don't eat up people's gardens, don't nest in corncribs, they don't do one thing but sing their hearts out for us. That's why it's a sin to kill a mockingbird.' Why is the word "sin" significant? What are the connotation and denotation of the word?

6. "Tim Johnson was advancing at a snail's pace, but he was not playing or sniffing at foliage: he seemed dedicated to one course and motivated by an invisible force that was inching him toward us. We could see him shiver like a horse shedding flies; his jaw opened and shut; he was alist, but he was being pulled gradually toward us." To what might the "invisible force" refer? Does it seem positive or negative? Why?

7. "'Atticus, you must be wrong. . .'
"How's that?"
"Well, most folks seem to think they're right and you're wrong. . ."
"They're certainly entitled to think that, and they're entitled to full respect for their opinions," said Atticus, "but before I can live with other folks I've got to live with myself. The one thing that doesn't abide by majority rule is a person's conscience." Look carefully at this passage and determine key words that are singular (you, I, myself, one, person's) and key words that are plural (most, folks, they're, majority). What tension is created in the passage by these singular and plural key words? Why does Scout believe that Atticus must be wrong? How does Atticus counter Scout's logic?

8. "I wanted you to see something about her—I wanted you to see what real courage is, instead of getting the idea that courage is a man with a gun in his hand. It's when you know you're licked before you begin but you begin anyway and you see it through no matter what. You rarely win, but sometimes you do. Mrs. Dubose won, all ninety-eight pounds of her. According to her views, she died beholden to nothing and nobody. She was the bravest person I ever knew."

To Kill A Mockingbird Chapters 8-11 Static and Dynamic Characters

A character can be either dynamic or static. A dynamic character grows or progresses in some way as plot in a story moves forward. A static character does not undergo a change and stays fundamentally the same.

From the list of characters below, put the names of dynamic characters in the relevant boxes and names of static characters in the relevant boxes. Complete the chart, using actual quotes when asked and noting page numbers. Go back and skim the text if you need to, to refresh your memory about these characters.

Scout | Heck Tate | Uncle Jack | Francis | Aunt Alexandra | Jem | Mrs. Dubose

Name of Dynamic Character	Quote – Observation 1 (Find a quote that shows how a character was before changing. Write the quote below.)	Quote – Observation 2 (Find a quote that shows how a character has undergone change. Write the quote below.)	Describe the Character's Change
Name of Static Character	Quote – Observation 1 (Find a quote that describes a quality or attitude of a static character. Write the quote below.)	Quote – Observation 2 (Find a quote later in the novel that shows that the character has the same quality or attitude. Write the quote below.)	Describe the Character's Quality or Attitude

To Kill A Mockingbird Chapters 8-11: Action, Character, Decision

Write **A** (for Action) **C** (for Character) or **D** (for Decision) in the blank next to each to identify whether the passage/statement advances the action, tells us more about a character, or provokes a decision. On the lines under each question, provide a short explanation of your choice.

___ 1. "The world's endin', Atticus! Please do something — !" I dragged him to the window and pointed.

___ 2. I looked down and found myself clutching a brown woolen blanket I was wearing around my shoulders, squaw-fashion.

___ 3. Rose Aylmer was Uncle Jack's cat. She was a beautiful yellow female Uncle Jack said was one of the few women he could stand permanently. He reached into his coat pocket and brought out some snapshots. We admired them.

___ 4. Jem said, "I reckon if he'd wanted us to know it, he'da told us. If he was proud of it, he'da told us."

"Maybe it just slipped his mind," I said.

"Naw, Scout, it's something you wouldn't understand. Atticus is real old, but I wouldn't care if he couldn't do anything — I wouldn't care if he couldn't do a blessed thing."

___ 5. But Mrs. Dubose held us: "Not only a Finch waiting on tables but one in the courthouse lawing for niggers!"

To Kill A Mockingbird Chapters 8-11: Figurative Language

Answer the questions that correspond to the letters on the lines below. Explain how the figurative language helps create meaning.

<u>Tim Johnson</u> (A) came into sight, walking dazedly in the inner rim of the curve parallel to the Radley house.

"Look at him," whispered Jem. "Mr. Heck said they walked in a straight line. <u>He can't even stay in the road</u> (B)."

"He looks more sick than anything," I said.

"Let anything get in front of him and he'll come straight at it."

Mr. Tate put his hand to his forehead and leaned forward. "He's got it all right, Mr. Finch."

<u>Tim Johnson was advancing at a snail's pace</u> (C), but he was not playing or sniffing at foliage: he seemed dedicated to one course and motivated by an invisible force that was inching him toward us. <u>We could see him shiver like a horse shedding flies</u> (D); his jaw opened and shut; he was alist, but he was being pulled gradually toward us.

"He's lookin' for a place to die," said Jem.

Mr. Tate turned around. "He's far from dead, Jem, he hasn't got started yet."

Tim Johnson reached the side street that ran in front of the Radley Place, and what remained of his poor mind made him pause and <u>seem to consider which road he would take</u> (E). He made a few hesitant steps and stopped in front of the Radley gate; then he tried to turn around, but was having difficulty.

A. The underlined section is what kind of figurative language?

_____

Why is the name "Tim Johnson" significant? Does it seem unusual? Why?

To Kill A Mockingbird Chapters 8-11: Figurative Language Page 2

B. The underlined section is what kind of figurative language?

_____

How does it contribute to meaning in the passage? What does it reveal about Jem?

_____
_____

C. The underlined section is what kind of figurative language?

_____

Why is the comparison significant?

_____
_____

D. The underlined section is what kind of figurative language?

_____

Why is the comparison significant? How is it related to Passage C?

_____
_____

E. The underlined section is what kind of figurative language?

_____

How does this particular action relate to larger themes in the novel?

_____
_____

To Kill A Mockingbird Chapters 8-11: Elements of Fiction & Literary Devices

1. One of the motifs in the novel is school, especially the first day of school. Consider this passage:

   My father looked at me mildly, amusement in his eyes. Despite our compromise, my campaign to avoid school had continued in one form or another since my first day's dose of it: the beginning of last September had brought on sinking spells, dizziness, and mild gastric complaints. I went so far as to pay a nickel for the privilege of rubbing my head against the head of Miss Rachel's cook's son, who was afflicted with a tremendous ringworm. It didn't take."

   How does Scout feel about school? Why does she go to such lengths to avoid it? What moral education does Scout receive at school?

2. What does Tim Johnson symbolize?

3. A motif in the novel is the concept of community. What community values are exhibited during the fire? What specific examples convey these values?

4. The role of women is a theme in the novel. How do various female characters influence Scout?

5. The titular mockingbird is a major symbol in the novel. What does it symbolize?

6. A major theme in the novel is courage. List examples of ways that characters have exhibited courage. Would these examples meet Atticus's definition of courage?

To Kill A Mockingbird Chapters 8-11: Meaning & Inferences 1

Read the passages and answer the related questions.

1. *"Miss Maudie stared down at me, her lips moving silently. Suddenly she put her hands to her head and whooped. When we left her, she was still chuckling.
Jem said he didn't know what was the matter with her — that was just Miss Maudie."*

What does this reveal about Miss Maudie's character? What is her state of mind?

2. *"He put his arms around me and rocked me gently. 'It's different this time,' he said. 'This time we aren't fighting the Yankees, we're fighting our friends. But remember this, no matter how bitter things get, they're still our friends and this is still our home.'"*

What is Atticus trying to convey to Scout? How are "Yankees" and "friends" different?

3. *"When supper was over, Uncle Jack went to the livingroom and sat down. He slapped his thighs for me to come sit on his lap. I liked to smell him: he was like a bottle of alcohol and something pleasantly sweet. He pushed back my bangs and looked at me. "You're more like Atticus than your mother," he said. "You're also growing out of your pants a little."*

How are Uncle Jack's observations also criticisms?

4. *"Why, I didn't think you'd hold it against me," he said. "I'm disappointed in you — you had that coming and you know it."*

Uncle Jack says this to Scout. Is he right? How does this show how different Uncle Jack is from Atticus?

5. *"I thought mad dogs foamed at the mouth, galloped, leaped and lunged at throats, and I thought they did it in August. Had Tim Johnson behaved thus, I would have been less frightened."*

What is Scout actually frightened by?

To Kill A Mockingbird Chapters 8-11: Meaning & Inferences 2

Read the passage and answer the related questions.

"If you shouldn't be defendin' him, then why are you doin' it?"

"For a number of reasons," said Atticus. "The main one is, if I didn't I couldn't hold up my head in town, I couldn't represent this county in the legislature, I couldn't even tell you or Jem not to do something again."

"You mean if you didn't defend that man, Jem and me wouldn't have to mind you any more?"

"That's about right."

"Why?"

"Because I could never ask you to mind me again. Scout, simply by the nature of the work, every lawyer gets at least one case in his lifetime that affects him personally. This one's mine, I guess. You might hear some ugly talk about it at school, but do one thing for me if you will: you just hold your head high and keep those fists down. No matter what anybody says to you, don't you let 'em get your goat. Try fighting with your head for a change. . . it's a good one, even if it does resist learning."

"Atticus, are we going to win it?"

"No, honey."

"Then why—"

"Simply because we were licked a hundred years before we started is no reason for us not to try to win," Atticus said.

1. What does Scout misunderstand about Atticus's defending Tom Robinson?

2. Why wouldn't Atticus be able to "hold up [his] head in town"?

3. To what is Atticus referring that happened "a hundred years before?" How is that affecting Atticus, Scout and the trial?

To Kill A Mockingbird Chapters 8-11: How Are Characters Prejudiced?

In chapters 8-11, as the plot advances and more tension begins to occur because of Atticus' role in the Tom Robinson trial, Harper Lee begins to explore the concept of prejudice through multiple characters.

Some of the characters who behave in a prejudicial way may be unaware of their prejudice, or they may feel fully entitled to their opinions. Look carefully at language and what characters say to one another. Are some statements deliberately prejudiced; are some inadvertent? As you look closely at the text, consider this difference. Does it matter? Does it relate to the characters' level of tolerance or open-mindedness? . Looking closely at the text for this deeper, additional meaning is called *critical reading,* a key skill for accomplished readers.

Using textual evidence from chapters 8-11, look for patterns to begin formulating an answer to the question "How are characters prejudiced?". As you develop an answer, consider why it is significant. Are there consequences to it? Who suffers those consequences?

To determine an idea about prejudice in the novel:

1. Identify passages and quotes where characters behave in a prejudiced way.

2. Examine the context of your quotes.

3. Consider the connotation and denotation of key phrases in your quotes.

    a. What is the tone—helpful, critical, angry, ignorant?
    b. Is there a perceived difference between the speaker and character addressed?
    c. What are the characters revealing or concealing in their language? Are they prejudiced?

4. Look for patterns in your evidence. Is a word or idea repeated? Use these patterns to shape an answer to the question.

To Kill A Mockingbird Chapters 8-11: How Are Characters Prejudiced?

Use this chart (and additional pages, if needed) to collect, analyze and evaluate information about characters' prejudice in the novel.

Quote (and page number)	Paraphrase Quote	What is the deeper meaning implied in quote?	How is prejudice occurring in the passage?	Why is this significant? Who is being negatively affected?

To Kill A Mockingbird Chapters 8-11: Creative Analytical Writing Assignments

1. Describe the night of the fire at Miss Maudie's from Boo Radley's perspective.

2. In the format of a play, write dialogue about a past Christmas at Finch's Landing when Scout and Francis got into a fight.

3. Write a story about when Atticus and Uncle Jack were boys and they received air rifles as a gift.

4. Write out a letter to Santa Claus from Scout. In the letter explain how she has been naughty and nice. Also include a list and descriptions of gifts she would like Santa Claus to bring her.

5. At multiple points, Atticus reminds Jem to behave like a gentleman. Write a description using quotes from the novel that explains what a gentleman is and how he behaves.

6. Write a guide for responsible use of an air rifle. Include relevant passages from the novel.

7. Find a passage in these chapters where "grown up" Scout is narrating. Rewrite the passage in the "present," from the perspective of young Scout.

8. Scout experiences fear multiple times in these chapters. Identify some moments when she is afraid. Write about these moments and explain if her fear is justified.

9. Atticus warns that killing a mockingbird is a sin. Is it? Write a brief definition of "sin," and then explain if killing a mockingbird qualifies as a sin by your definition.

10. Imagine that Atticus makes Jem speak at Mrs. Dubose's funeral. Write a brief eulogy that sums up Jem's feelings towards her.

To Kill A Mockingbird Chapters 8-11: Quick-Write Writing Assignments

1. A motif in the novel is seasons. Why is it significant that Maycomb is experiencing an unusually cold winter? Why is it significant that the fire occurs on the "night of the deep freeze"?

2. What is Miss Maudie's response to the fire? Why do the children find it unexpected?

3. Describe Tom Robinson. What is Atticus's attitude toward him?

4. How are Francis and Scout similar? How are they different?

5. What is the history of Finch's Landing? Why is this detail significant? Does it influence how readers view Atticus?

6. Does Uncle Jack treat Scout fairly?

7. Why is Atticus so modest?

8. Is Atticus a good parent?

9. What does Miss Maudie mean by "unfair advantage?"

10. Explain Jem's reaction to the boxed camellia bloom.

Notes
To Kill A Mockingbird

MATERIALS: CHAPTERS 12-14
TO KILL A MOCKINGBIRD

Reading Activity 1: True or False

Reading Activity 2: Analyzing Passages

Reading Activity 3: Characters Who Are Foils

Reading Activity 4: Action, Character, Decision

Reading Activity 5: Figurative Language

Reading Activity 6: Elements of Fiction & Literary Devices

Reading Activity 7: Meaning and Inferences

Writing Activity 1: Who is Calpurnia?

Suggested Writing Assignments

Quick-Write Assignments

NOTES
To Kill A Mockingbird

To Kill A Mockingbird Chapters 12-14: True or False?

Write *True* or *False* in the blank next to each statement. Below the statement, explain why you chose true or false, referencing the text to support your choices.

_____ 1. Jem sees Scout as his equal.

_____ 2. Scout is not aware of her socio-economic status in Maycomb society.

_____ 3. Calpurnia is not like most other black people in Maycomb.

To Kill A Mockingbird Chapters 12-14 True or False Worksheet Page 2

_____ 4. Aunt Alexandra is honest and fair.

_____ 5. Atticus has a clear sense of which values he wants to teach his children.

_____ 6. Dill feels lonely and unwanted.

To Kill A Mockingbird Chapters 12-14 True or False Evaluation

List Your Group's Members: Your Group's Question # _____

_____   _____   _____

_____   _____   _____

    1 = No, Not At All   **2** = A Little   **3** = Some   **4** = Yes   **5** = Yes, Very Well

Evaluation of Question # ___
Does the explanation support the answer of true or false?	1 2 3 4 5
Is there good textual evidence to support the answer?	1 2 3 4 5
Is the answer clearly stated?	1 2 3 4 5

                             Total Score _____ of a possible 15 points

Evaluation of Question # ___
Does the explanation support the answer of true or false?	1 2 3 4 5
Is there good textual evidence to support the answer?	1 2 3 4 5
Is the answer clearly stated?	1 2 3 4 5

                             Total Score _____ of a possible 15 points

Evaluation of Question # ___
Does the explanation support the answer of true or false?	1 2 3 4 5
Is there good textual evidence to support the answer?	1 2 3 4 5
Is the answer clearly stated?	1 2 3 4 5

                             Total Score _____ of a possible 15 points

Evaluation of Question # ___
Does the explanation support the answer of true or false?	1 2 3 4 5
Is there good textual evidence to support the answer?	1 2 3 4 5
Is the answer clearly stated?	1 2 3 4 5

                             Total Score _____ of a possible 15 points

Evaluation of Question # ___
Does the explanation support the answer of true or false?	1 2 3 4 5
Is there good textual evidence to support the answer?	1 2 3 4 5
Is the answer clearly stated?	1 2 3 4 5

                             Total Score _____ of a possible 15 points

To Kill A Mockingbird Chapters 12-14 Analyzing Passages

Answer the questions following the quotations completely.

1. "First Purchase African M.E. Church was in the Quarters outside the southern town limits, across the old sawmill tracks. It was an ancient paint-peeled frame building, the only church in Maycomb with a steeple and bell, called First Purchase because it was paid for from the first earnings of freed slaves. Negroes worshiped in it on Sundays and white men gambled in it on weekdays."

What contradictions are present in the passage? Why are they significant?

2. "That Calpurnia led a modest double life never dawned on me. The idea that she had a separate existence outside our household was a novel one, to say nothing of her having command of two languages.
    'Cal,' I asked, 'why do you talk nigger- talk to the — to your folks when you know it's not right?'"

Do Scout's thoughts or dialogue reveal prejudice? How, specifically?

3. "I could think of nothing else to say to her. In fact I could never think of anything to say to her, and I sat thinking of past painful conversations between us: How are you, Jean Louise? Fine, thank you ma'am, how are you? Very well, thank you, what have you been doing with yourself? Nothin'. Don't you do anything? Nome. Certainly you have friends? Yessum. Well what do you all do? Nothin'."

Are these reflections from "grown up" Scout or from young Scout in the present moment of the novel? Does it matter? How would that change meaning?

To Kill A Mockingbird Chapters 12-14 Analyzing Passages Page 2

4. "Atticus answered both questions in the affirmative. 'How'd you like for her to come live with us?'
   I said I would like it very much, which was a lie, but one must lie under certain circumstances and at all times when one can't do anything about them."
Does this statement seem congruent with how Scout usually behaves?

5. "To all parties present and participating in the life of the county, Aunt Alexandra was one of the last of her kind: she had river-boat, boarding-school manners; let any moral come along and she would uphold it; she was born in the objective case; she was an incurable gossip. When Aunt Alexandra went to school, self-doubt could not be found in any textbook, so she knew not its meaning. She was never bored, and given the slightest chance she would exercise her royal prerogative: she would arrange, advise, caution, and warn."
Is this description primarily positive or negative?

6. "I never understood her preoccupation with heredity. Somewhere, I had received the impression that Fine Folks were people who did the best they could with the sense they had, but Aunt Alexandra was of the opinion, obliquely expressed, that the longer a family had been squatting on one patch of land the finer it was."
Consider the double meaning of the word "fine." What implications does it create?

To Kill A Mockingbird Chapters 12-14 Analyzing Passages Page 3

7. "'Besides, I don't think the children've suffered one bit from her having brought them up. If anything, she's been harder on them in some ways than a mother would have been. . . she's never let them get away with anything, she's never indulged them the way most colored nurses do. She tried to bring them up according to her lights, and Cal's lights are pretty good — and another thing, the children love her.'"
What does Atticus value about Calpurnia's care?

8. "'Why do you reckon Boo Radley's never run off?' Dill sighed a long sigh and turned away from me.
   'Maybe he doesn't have anywhere to run off to. . .'
What does Dill's response reveal about him? What might he have in common with Boo Radley?

To Kill A Mockingbird Chapters 12-14: Characters Who Are Foils

A character in a work of fiction can be a foil to another character, presented as a contrast to emphasize a quality or to show some advantage or difference.

Complete the chart, using actual quotes when asked and noting page numbers. Go back and skim the text if you need to, to refresh your memory about these characters.

Character Name and Description	Foil Name and Description	What qualities, difference or advantage do they highlight in one another?	Why is this significant?
Aunt Alexandra	Calpurnia		
Calpurnia	Lula		
Scout	Dill		

To Kill A Mockingbird Chapters 12-14: Action, Character, Decision

Write **A** (for Action) **C** (for Character) or **D** (for Decision) in the blank next to each to identify whether the passage/statement advances the action, tells us more about a character, or provokes a decision. On the lines under each question, provide a short explanation of your choice.

___ 1. "Enarmored, upright, uncompromising, Aunt Alexandra was sitting in a rocking chair exactly as if she had sat there every day of her life."

___ 2. "Calpurnia picked up Aunty's heavy suitcase and opened the door. 'I'll take it,' said Jem, and took it."

___ 3. "I don't want you to remember it. Forget it."

___ 4. "I remembered something. 'Yessum, and she promised me I could come out to her house some afternoon. Atticus, I'll go next Sunday if it's all right, can I? Cal said she'd come get me if you were off in the car.'

'You may not.'

Aunt Alexandra said it."

___ 5. "By an involved route. Refreshed by food, Dill recited this narrative: having been bound in chains and left to die in the basement (there were basements in Meridian) by his new father, who disliked him, and secretly kept alive on raw field peas by a passing farmer who heard his cries for help (the good man poked a bushel pod by pod through the ventilator), Dill worked himself free by pulling the chains from the wall. Still in wrist manacles, he wandered two miles out of Meridian where he discovered a small animal show and was immediately engaged to wash the camel. He traveled with the show all over Mississippi until his infallible sense of direction told him he was in Abbott County, Alabama, just across the river from Maycomb. He walked the rest of the way."

To Kill A Mockingbird Chapters 12-14: Figurative Language

Answer the questions below. Explain how the figurative language helps create meaning.

Dill's voice was his own again: "Oh, they ain't mean. They kiss you and hug you good night and good mornin' and good-bye and tell you they love you — Scout, let's get us a baby."

"Where?"

There was a man Dill had heard of who had a boat that he rowed across to a foggy island where all these babies were; you could order one —

"That's a lie. Aunty said God drops 'em down the chimney. At least that's what I think she said." For once, Aunty's diction had not been too clear.

"Well that ain't so. You get babies from each other. But there's this man, too — he has all these babies just waitin' to wake up, he breathes life into 'em. . ."

Dill was off again. Beautiful things floated around in his dreamy head. He could read two books to my one, but he preferred the magic of his own inventions. He could add and subtract faster than lightning, but he preferred his own twilight world, a world where babies slept, waiting to be gathered like morning lilies. He was slowly talking himself to sleep and taking me with him, but in the quietness of his foggy island there rose the faded image of a gray house with sad brown doors.

A. What is euphemism?
_____

B. Why is euphemism a useful rhetorical tool?
_____

C. While the speakers in the passage may be unaware that they are using euphemisms because they are young and innocent, how does Harper Lee use euphemism here? To what is she alluding?
_____
_____
_____

D. Why is Scout's observation about "Aunty's diction" significant? What does it reveal about Aunt Alexandra and her attitude toward the subject?
_____
_____
_____

E. How does the use of euphemism affect the mood of the passage?
_____
_____

To Kill a Mockingbird Chapters 12-14:
Elements of Fiction & Literary Devices

Answer the questions below and refer to the scene in chapter 12 where Jem and Scout accompany Calpurnia to church.

1. A church is usually thought of as a sacred and holy place. Does this description fit the First Purchase African M.E. Church? Use examples from the text.

2. Look at the descriptive passage below. What is interesting about it? Why all the sensory descriptions? What mood do they create?

> The churchyard was brick-hard clay, as was the cemetery beside it. If someone died during a dry spell, the body was covered with chunks of ice until rain softened the earth. A few graves in the cemetery were marked with crumbling tombstones; newer ones were outlined with brightly colored glass and broken Coca-Cola bottles. Lightning rods guarding some graves denoted dead who rested uneasily; stumps of burned-out candles stood at the heads of infant graves. It was a happy cemetery.
>
> The warm bittersweet smell of clean Negro welcomed us as we entered the churchyard — Hearts of Love hairdressing mingled with asafoetida, snuff, Hoyt's Cologne, Brown's Mule, peppermint, and lilac talcum.

3. Some characters are out of place in some settings. Are Jem and Scout out of place at the First Purchase African M.E. Church? Include quotes and examples in your answer.

4. How does the setting affect Calpurnia?

To Kill a Mockingbird Chapters 12-14 Elements of Fiction & Literary Devices Page 2

5. What do Jem and Scout notice about the church experience that is different from their usual experience in church? What do they think about these differences?

6. Why is the collection significant? How does it relate to other issues in the novel?

To Kill A Mockingbird Chapters 12-14: Meaning & Inferences 1

Read the passages and answer the related questions.

1. *"I looked over to the Radley Place, expecting to see its phantom occupant sunning himself in the swing. The swing was empty."*

Who is the "phantom occupant"?

2. *There was indeed a caste system in Maycomb, but to my mind it worked this way: the older citizens, the present generation of people who had lived side by side for years and years, were utterly predictable to one another: they took for granted attitudes, character shadings, even gestures, as having been repeated in each generation and refined by time.*

What is the "caste system"? How does it actually work?

3. *"Aunt Alexandra fitted into the world of Maycomb like a hand into a glove, but never into the world of Jem and me."*

What does this suggest about the relationship of "the world of Maycomb" to Jem and Scout?

4. *"I know now what he was trying to do, but Atticus was only a man. It takes a woman to do that kind of work"*

To what "kind of work" is the narrator referring?

5. *"Then he rose and broke the remaining code of our childhood."*

What is the "code of our childhood"?

To Kill A Mockingbird Chapters 12-14: Meaning & Inferences 2

Read the passage and answer the related questions.

Aunt Alexandra, in underlining the moral of young Sam Merriweather's suicide, said it was caused by a morbid streak in the family. Let a sixteen-year-old girl giggle in the choir and Aunty would say, "It just goes to show you, all the Penfield women are flighty." Everybody in Maycomb, it seemed, had a Streak: a Drinking Streak, a Gambling Streak, a Mean Streak, a Funny Streak.

Once, when Aunty assured us that Miss Stephanie Crawford's tendency to mind other people's business was hereditary, Atticus said, "Sister, when you stop to think about it, our generation's practically the first in the Finch family not to marry its cousins. Would you say the Finches have an Incestuous Streak?"

Aunty said no, that's where we got our small hands and feet.

I never understood her preoccupation with heredity. Somewhere, I had received the impression that Fine Folks were people who did the best they could with the sense they had, but Aunt Alexandra was of the opinion, obliquely expressed, that the longer a family had been squatting on one patch of land the finer it was.

"That makes the Ewells fine folks, then," said Jem. The tribe of which Burris Ewell and his brethren consisted had lived on the same plot of earth behind the Maycomb dump, and had thrived on county welfare money for three generations.

1. What does "hereditary" mean for Aunt Alexandra?

2. Evaluate the tone of Atticus's question. Is he serious?

3. How does Jem's logic disprove Aunt Alexandra's ideas?

4. What implications does Aunt Alexandra's thought about family "streaks" have? Is Aunt Alexandra capable of seeing people as individuals?

5. Do you think Atticus, Jem and Scout agree with Aunt Alexandra's ideas? Why is this ironic?

To Kill a Mockingbird Chapters 12-14: Who Is Calpurnia?

These chapters offer an important glimpse into Maycomb's black community. The chapters also reveal more about Calpurnia and use her character as a bridge between these two distinct cultures.

Details in fiction are hardly accidents, but instead are ways to build characterization in subtle ways. Close reading of detail can uncover layers of meaning important to understanding a novel's themes.

Using textual evidence from chapters 12-14, look for important but perhaps seemingly insignificant details to answer to the question: Who is Calpurnia?

To explore Calpurnia's character:

1. Identify passages and quotes which offer details or insights into Calpurnia.

2. Examine the context of your quotes.

3. Consider the connotation and denotation of key phrases in your quotes.

   a. What information is offered by Calpurnia?
   b. What do the children ask Calpurnia? Does she offer responses?
   c. What do the children learn that they did not know about her?
   d. What do other characters say about her?
   e. How does Calpurnia "belong" to two different worlds?

To Kill a Mockingbird Chapters 12-14: Who Is Calpurnia?

Use this chart (and additional pages, if needed) to collect, analyze and evaluate information about Calpurnia.

Quote (and page number)	Paraphrase Quote	What does this reveal about Calpurnia?	Why is this significant?

To Kill a Mockingbird Chapters 12-14: Creative Analytical Writing Assignments

1. Write a letter from Scout to Dill explaining why she will miss his summer visit.

2. Write a scene in dialogue of a conversation between Helen Robinson and Calpurnia. Express the problems Helen is facing.

3. Jem and Scout continue to grow apart as Jem matures. Write about moments in the text which illustrate this growing distance and explain in what ways Jem is changing.

4. Atticus says that the children love Calpurnia. Find moments in the text that prove this statement. In what ways do the children demonstrate their love for Calpurnia?

5. Reading is an activity important to the Finch family. Describe Scout's response when she learns that most people at the First Purchase Church are illiterate.

6. Write about Aunt Alexandra's view of "streaks" in families. Is her logic sound or is it flawed?

7. Write a story about when Atticus and Aunt Alexandra were children. Emphasize the dominant aspects of their personalities.

8. Describe the "caste system" in Maycomb from Aunt Alexandra's perspective, Scout's perspective, and Atticus's perspective.

9. Explain why Atticus is preoccupied with state legislature affairs. What, historically, is happening during this time period? How does it affect meaning in the novel?

10. Aunt Alexandra hopes to influence Scout. Write a description using quotes from the novel that explains what a lady is and how she behaves.

To Kill a Mockingbird Chapters 12-14: Quick-Write Writing Assignments

1. Explain the political cartoon Atticus describes in chapter 12.
2. Why is the topic of Reverend Sykes's sermon significant? How does it relate to other themes in the novel?
3. What is the book *Blackstone's Commentaries*? Why is it an unusual book for a beginning learner?
4. What does "live up to your name" mean?
5. What are some ways that Atticus is very transparent with his children?
6. Why is Aunt Alexandra against Scout visiting Calpurnia's house?
7. How has losing their mother affected Jem and Scout?
8. Is Alexandra's desire to terminate Calpurnia's employment justified? Is it a good or bad idea?
9. Why does Dill exaggerate so much?
10. Why hasn't Boo run off?

Notes
To Kill A Mockingbird

MATERIALS: CHAPTERS 15-21
TO KILL A MOCKINGBIRD

Reading Activity 1: True or False

Reading Activity 2: Analyzing Passages

Reading Activity 3: Direct and Indirect Characterization

Reading Activity 4: Action, Character, Decision

Reading Activity 5: Figurative Language

Reading Activity 6: Elements of Fiction & Literary Devices

Reading Activity 7: Meaning and Inferences

Writing Activity 1: What Is The Purpose Of The trial?

Suggested Writing Assignments

Quick-Write Assignments

NOTES
To Kill A Mockingbird

To Kill A Mockingbird Chapters 15-21: True or False?

Write *True* or *False* in the blank next to each statement. Below the statement, explain why you chose true or false, referencing the text to support your choices.

_____ 1. Atticus underestimates the threat of violence that the trial poses to him and the community.

_____ 2. Bob Ewell cares about his daughter's safety.

_____ 3. Jem and Scout do not share the same attitude about race as most other white residents of Maycomb.

To Kill A Mockingbird Chapters 15-21 True or False? Worksheet Page 2

_____ 4. Mayella Ewell is willing to do the right thing and admit her lie.

_____ 5. Dolphus Raymond is not what he appears to be.

_____ 6. Jem understands that Atticus was "licked" before he began.

To Kill A Mockingbird Chapters 15-21 True or False? Evaluation

List Your Group's Members:　　　　　　Your Group's Question # _____

_____　　_____　　_____

_____　　_____　　_____

　　　1 = No, Not At All　　**2** = A Little　　**3** = Some　　**4** = Yes　　**5** = Yes, Very Well

Evaluation of Question # ___
Does the explanation support the answer of true or false?	1　2　3　4　5
Is there good textual evidence to support the answer?	1　2　3　4　5
Is the answer clearly stated?	1　2　3　4　5

　　　　　　　　　　　　　Total Score _____ of a possible 15 points

Evaluation of Question # ___
Does the explanation support the answer of true or false?	1　2　3　4　5
Is there good textual evidence to support the answer?	1　2　3　4　5
Is the answer clearly stated?	1　2　3　4　5

　　　　　　　　　　　　　Total Score _____ of a possible 15 points

Evaluation of Question # ___
Does the explanation support the answer of true or false?	1　2　3　4　5
Is there good textual evidence to support the answer?	1　2　3　4　5
Is the answer clearly stated?	1　2　3　4　5

　　　　　　　　　　　　　Total Score _____ of a possible 15 points

Evaluation of Question # ___
Does the explanation support the answer of true or false?	1　2　3　4　5
Is there good textual evidence to support the answer?	1　2　3　4　5
Is the answer clearly stated?	1　2　3　4　5

　　　　　　　　　　　　　Total Score _____ of a possible 15 points

Evaluation of Question # ___
Does the explanation support the answer of true or false?	1　2　3　4　5
Is there good textual evidence to support the answer?	1　2　3　4　5
Is the answer clearly stated?	1　2　3　4　5

　　　　　　　　　　　　　Total Score _____ of a possible 15 points

To Kill A Mockingbird Chapters 15-21: Analyzing Passages

Answer the questions following the quotations completely.

1. "I sought Jem and found him in his room, on the bed deep in thought. "Have they been at it?" I asked.

   "Sort of. She won't let him alone about Tom Robinson. She almost said Atticus was disgracin' the family. Scout... I'm scared."

   "Scared'a what?"

   "Scared about Atticus. Somebody might hurt him." Jem preferred to remain mysterious; all he would say to my questions was go on and leave him alone.
   Why does Jem "remain mysterious"?

2. "So it took an eight-year-old child to bring 'em to their senses, didn't it?" said Atticus. "That proves something — that a gang of wild animals can be stopped, simply because they're still human. Hmp, maybe we need a police force of children. . . you children last night made Walter Cunningham stand in my shoes for a minute. That was enough."
   What "was enough"?

3. "The Maycomb County courthouse...pillars were all that remained standing when the original courthouse burned in 1856. Another courthouse was built around them. It is better to say, built in spite of them. But for the south porch, the Maycomb County courthouse was early Victorian, presenting an unoffensive vista when seen from the north. From the other side, however, Greek revival columns clashed with a big nineteenth-century clock tower housing a rusty unreliable instrument, a view indicating a people determined to preserve every physical scrap of the past."

To Kill A Mockingbird Chapters 15-21 Analyzing Passages Page 2

4. "'There has been a request,' Judge Taylor said, 'that this courtroom be cleared of spectators, or at least of women and children, a request that will be denied for the time being. People generally see what they look for, and hear what they listen for, and they have the right to subject their children to it, but I can assure you of one thing: you will receive what you see and hear in silence or you will leave this courtroom, but you won't leave it until the whole boiling of you come before me on contempt charges.'"
Why is this ironic?

5. "Suddenly Mayella became articulate. 'I got somethin' to say,' she said.

Atticus raised his head. 'Do you want to tell us what happened?'

But she did not hear the compassion in his invitation. 'I got somethin' to say an' then I ain't gonna say no more. That nigger yonder took advantage of me an' if you fine fancy gentlemen don't wanta do nothin' about it then you're all yellow stinkin' cowards, stinkin' cowards, the lot of you. Your fancy airs don't come to nothin' — your ma'amin' and Miss Mayellerin' don't come to nothin', Mr. Finch."

6. "She was white, and she tempted a Negro. She did something that in our society is unspeakable: she kissed a black man. Not an old Uncle, but a strong young Negro man. No code mattered to her before she broke it, but it came crashing down on her afterwards."
What does Atticus mean by "code"?

7. "'Which, gentlemen, we know is in itself a lie as black as Tom Robinson's skin, a lie I do not have to point out to you. You know the truth, and the truth is this: some Negroes lie, some Negroes are immoral, some Negro men are not to be trusted around women—black or white. But this is a truth that applies to the human race and to no particular race of men. There is not a person in this courtroom who has never told a lie, who has never done an immoral thing, and there is no man living who has never looked upon a woman without desire.'"
Explain the logic of Atticus's argument.

8. "What happened after that had a dreamlike quality: in a dream I saw the jury return, moving like underwater swimmers, and Judge Taylor's voice came from far away and was tiny. I saw something only a lawyer's child could be expected to see, could be expected to watch for, and it was like watching Atticus walk into the street, raise a rifle to his shoulder and pull the trigger, but watching all the time knowing that the gun was empty."
Explain the allusion to the Tim Johnson incident.

To Kill A Mockingbird Chapters 15-21: Direct vs. Indirect Characterization

Characterization, or the development of characters in a work of fiction, can be direct or indirect. Direct characterization is revealing aspects of character directly to the reader via a narrator, the character him or herself or from another character. Indirect characterization requires readers to infer what a character is like through the character's thoughts, action, diction, appearance and interactions with others.

Complete the chart, using actual quotes when asked and noting page numbers.

Character	Direct Characterization Quote	Indirect Characterization Quote	Indirect Characterization Inference
Judge Taylor			
Horace Gilmer			
Bob Ewell			
Mayella Ewell			
Dolphus Raymond			
Reverand Sykes			

To Kill A Mockingbird Chapters 15-21: Action, Character, Decision

Write **A** (for Action) **C** (for Character) or **D** (for Decision) in the blank next to each to identify whether the passage/statement advances the action, tells us more about a character, or provokes a decision. On the lines under each question, provide a short explanation of your choice.

___ 1. "'Don't be foolish, Heck,' Atticus said. 'This is Maycomb.'"

___ 2. "'He's in my grade,' I said, 'and he does right well. He's a good boy,' I added, 'a real nice boy. We brought him home for dinner one time. Maybe he told you about me, I beat him up one time but he was real nice about it. Tell him hey for me, won't you?'"

___ 3. "'I am not. 't's morbid, watching a poor devil on trial for his life. Look at all those folks, it's like a Roman carnival.'"

___ 4. "She reached up an' kissed me 'side of th' face. She says she never kissed a grown man before an' she might as well kiss a nigger. She says what her papa do to her don't count. She says, 'Kiss me back, nigger.' I say Miss Mayella lemme outa here an' tried to run but she got her back to the door an' I'da had to push her. I didn't wanta harm her, Mr. Finch, an' I say lemme pass, but just when I say it Mr. Ewell yonder hollered through th' window."

___ 5. "In the name of God, believe him,' I think that's what he said."

To Kill A Mockingbird Chapters 15-21: Figurative Language

Contextualize and explain the passages below. Explain how irony helps create meaning. Irony is the contrast between what is expected or what appears to be and what actually is.

1. Hmp, maybe we need a police force of children. . .

   _____
   _____
   _____

2. Dill was encumbered by the chair, and his pace was slower. Atticus and Jem were well ahead of us, and I assumed that Atticus was giving him hell for not going home, but I was wrong. As they passed under a streetlight, Atticus reached out and massaged Jem's hair, his one gesture of affection.

   _____
   _____
   _____

3. Why don't you drink your coffee, Scout?"

   _____
   _____
   _____

4. Uncle Jack Finch says we really don't know. He says as far as he can trace back the Finches we ain't, but for all he knows we mighta come straight out of Ethiopia durin' the Old Testament."

   "Well if we came out durin' the Old Testament it's too long ago to matter."

   "That's what I thought," said Jem, "but around here once you have a drop of Negro blood, that makes you all black. Hey, look — "

   _____
   _____
   _____

5. One corner of the yard, though, bewildered Maycomb. Against the fence, in a line, were six chipped-enamel slop jars holding brilliant red geraniums, cared for as tenderly as if they belonged to Miss Maudie Atkinson, had Miss Maudie deigned to permit a geranium on her premises.

   _____
   _____
   _____

To Kill A Mockingbird Chapters 15-21: Elements of Fiction & Literary Devices

All fiction is based on conflict, which propels plot forward. Conflict is the problem or struggle in a work of fiction that prompts action. There are five basic types of conflict: person vs. person, person vs. society, person vs. self, person vs. nature, person vs. fate. Answer the questions below.

1. Explain how the divergent opinions between Atticus and Aunt Alexandra are an example of person vs. person conflict.

2. Explain how a guilty verdict against Tom Robinson is a person vs. society conflict.

3. Explain how Mayella has a person vs. self conflict.

4. Explain how "heredity," as Aunt Alexandra explains it, is a person vs. nature conflict.

5. Explain how Atticus's representing Tom Robinson is an example of a man vs. fate conflict.

To Kill A Mockingbird Chapters 15-21: Meaning & Inferences 1

Read the passages and answer the related questions.

1. "...in favor of Southern womanhood as much as anybody, but not for preserving polite fiction at the expense of human life," a pronouncement that made me suspect they had been fussing again.

What does "Southern womanhood" mean here? What is Atticus saying about it?

2. "It was just him I couldn't stand," Dill said...."That old Mr. Gilmer doin' him thataway, talking so hateful to him...It was the way he said it made me sick, plain sick.... The way that man called him 'boy' all the time an' sneered at him, an' looked around at the jury every time he answered...It ain't right, somehow it ain't right to do 'em that way. Hasn't anybody got any business talkin' like that—it just makes me sick."

What is Dill criticizing?

3. "'But you weren't in a fix—you testified that you were resisting Miss Ewell. Were you so scared that she'd hurt you, you ran, a big buck like you?'
'No suh, I's scared I'd be in court, just like I am now.'
'Scared of arrest, scared you'd have to face up to what you did?'
'No suh, scared I'd hafta face up to what I didn't do.'"

What is Tom scared of? What does this reveal about the way black men are treated in Maycomb?

4. "But why had he entrusted us with his deepest secret? I asked him why.
'Because you're children and you can understand it,' he said, 'and because I heard that one-'
He jerked his head at Dill: 'Things haven't caught up with that one's instinct yet. Let him get a little older and he won't get sick and cry. Maybe things'll strike him as being—not quite right, say, but he won't cry, not when he gets a few years on him.'"

Who is the speaker? What is the speaker inferring about children, and about Dill, specifically?

5. *"Someone was punching me, but I was reluctant to take my eyes from the people below us, and from the image of Atticus's lonely walk down the aisle.*

   'Miss Jean Louise?'

   I looked around. They were standing. All around us and in the balcony on the opposite wall, the Negroes were getting to their feet. Reverend Sykes's voice was as distant as Judge Taylor's:

   'Miss Jean Louise, stand up. Your father's passin'.'"

Why do the people stand?

To Kill A Mockingbird Chapters 15-21: Meaning & Inferences 2

Read the passage and answer the related questions.

"Hey, Mr. Cunningham."

The man did not hear me, it seemed.

"Hey, Mr. Cunningham. How's your entailment gettin' along?"

Mr. Walter Cunningham's legal affairs were well known to me; Atticus had once described them at length. The big man blinked and hooked his thumbs in his overall straps. He seemed uncomfortable; he cleared his throat and looked away. My friendly overture had fallen flat.

Mr. Cunningham wore no hat, and the top half of his forehead was white in contrast to his sunscorched face, which led me to believe that he wore one most days. He shifted his feet, clad in heavy work shoes.

"Don't you remember me, Mr. Cunningham? I'm Jean Louise Finch. You brought us some hickory nuts one time, remember?" I began to sense the futility one feels when unacknowledged by a chance acquaintance.

"I go to school with Walter," I began again. "He's your boy, ain't he? Ain't he, sir?"

Mr. Cunningham was moved to a faint nod. He did know me, after all.

"He's in my grade," I said, "and he does right well. He's a good boy," I added, "a real nice boy. We brought him home for dinner one time. Maybe he told you about me, I beat him up one time but he was real nice about it. Tell him hey for me, won't you?"

1. Why is Mr. Cunningham "uncomfortable"?

2. Cite some examples of how Scout creates a personal connection with Mr. Cunningham.

3. Is Scout correct that she is being ignored?

4. Most of Scout's dialogue to Mr. Cunningham is in the form of questions. What rhetorical effect does this have?

5. Explain how Scout's mention of her fight with Walter is ironic.

To Kill a Mockingbird Chapters 15-21: What Is The Purpose Of The Trial?

As Atticus explains about Mrs. Dubose's struggle to overcome her morphine addiction, a courageous act is one when you begin knowing that you are already "licked." This applies to Tom Robinson's trial and Atticus's defense of Tom. Yet, the trial must proceed anyway even though the outcome is virtually guaranteed. These chapters show the unfolding action of the trial and its inevitable conclusion, but the trial has other effects and consequences.

Through close reading of the text, determine how the trial affected various audiences as well as the reader.

Using textual evidence from chapters 15-21, look for important but perhaps seemingly insignificant details to answer to the question: What is the purpose of the trial?

To explore the point of the trial:

1. Identify passages and quotes which offer details or insights into how various audiences view the trial.

2. Examine the context of your quotes.

3. Consider the connotation and denotation of key phrases in your quotes.

    a. Do characters express opinions about the trial or its outcome?
    b. How have characters been affected?
    c. Do the phrases suggest a change in attitude or opinion?
    d. Consider the reader's perspective as an observer of the trial. What themes does the trial elucidate for the reader? How?

4. Review passages for patterns to determine what purpose the trial has for the audience?

To Kill a Mockingbird Chapters 15-21: What Is The Purpose Of The Trial?

Use this chart (and additional pages, if needed) to collect, analyze and evaluate information about the trial.

Audience	In their view, who or what is on trial? Include textual evidence and page numbers.	In their view, how just is the verdict? Include textual evidence and page numbers.	What does the verdict affect them? What is the purpose of the trial? Include textual evidence and page numbers.
White residents of Maycomb			
Black residents of Maycomb			
Children (as represented by Scout, Jem, Dill)			
The reader			

To Kill A Mockingbird Chapters 15-21:
Creative Analytical Writing Assignments

1. Write a scene where Mr. Gilmer meets with Bob Ewell and Mayella Ewell to prepare them for their witness testimony. Mr. Gilmer is trying to help them clarify their accounts of the event.

2. Write a newspaper article by Mr. Underwood about the trial. Incorporate quotes from the novel into your article.

3. Which characters do not attend the trial or sit in the main area reserved for white people? What do these characters have in common? Explain their shared characteristics in a paragraph/essay.

4. In what ways is the trial salacious? How does Judge Taylor handle this? Include examples from the text.

5. Write an outline of Atticus's legal strategy.

6. Write a scene in the form of dialogue that explains how the jurors reached their verdict.

7. If Dolphus Raymond has created a "story" to help others "understand" his choices, what other characters might create "stories" as well?

8. Imagine Dill at some point in the future. Describe his attitude towards race.

9. Write a "missing scene" where Atticus has a private conversation with Tom Robinson after the verdict is delivered.

10. Dolphus Raymond's children are described as not belonging to the white community or the black community. Which other characters subvert convention and do not necessarily belong to an "expected" category?

To Kill A Mockingbird Chapters 15-21: Quick-Write Writing Assignments

1. Is Atticus scared? If so, of what? If not, should he be?
2. Why doesn't Miss Maudie go to the trial?
3. Why is the name Robert E. Lee Ewell significant?
4. Why is it significant that the children are in the balcony during the trial?
5. What is the atmosphere at the trial like?
6. Is Mr. Gilmer a good lawyer?
7. Why does Dill cry?
8. Is Mayella a victim?
9. Why is Aunt Alexandra sad when the children return home to eat?
10. What is the source of Jem's idealism?

MATERIALS: CHAPTERS 22-31
TO KILL A MOCKINGBIRD

Reading Activity 1: True or False

Reading Activity 2: Analyzing Passages

Reading Activity 3: Round Character or Stereotype?

Reading Activity 4: Action, Character, Decision

Reading Activity 5: Figurative Language

Reading Activity 6: Elements of Fiction & Literary Devices

Reading Activity 7: Meaning and Inferences

Writing Activity 1: Significance Of Tom Robinson's & Boo Radley's Similarities

Suggested Writing Assignments

Quick-Write Assignments

Notes
To Kill A Mockingbird

To Kill A Mockingbird Chapters 22-31: True or False?

Write *True* or *False* in the blank next to each statement. Below the statement, explain why you chose true or false, referencing the text to support your choices.

_____ 1. Atticus is afraid of Bob Ewell.

_____ 2. Tom Robinson is optimistic that he will be pardoned.

_____ 3. The Cunninghams are good, moral people.

To Kill A Mockingbird Chapters 22-31 True or False? Page 2

_____ 4. Many women in the missionary circle are hypocrites.

_____ 5. Bob Ewell goes to prison for his bad behavior.

_____ 6. Scout and Boo begin a long friendship and companionship.

To Kill A Mockingbird Chapters 22-31 True or False Evaluation

List Your Group's Members: Your Group's Question # _____

_____   _____   _____

_____   _____   _____

1 = No, Not At All   **2** = A Little   **3** = Some   **4** = Yes   **5** = Yes, Very Well

Evaluation of Question # ___
Does the explanation support the answer of true or false?   1   2   3   4   5
Is there good textual evidence to support the answer?   1   2   3   4   5
Is the answer clearly stated?   1   2   3   4   5
                 Total Score _____ of a possible 15 points

Evaluation of Question # ___
Does the explanation support the answer of true or false?   1   2   3   4   5
Is there good textual evidence to support the answer?   1   2   3   4   5
Is the answer clearly stated?   1   2   3   4   5
                 Total Score _____ of a possible 15 points

Evaluation of Question # ___
Does the explanation support the answer of true or false?   1   2   3   4   5
Is there good textual evidence to support the answer?   1   2   3   4   5
Is the answer clearly stated?   1   2   3   4   5
                 Total Score _____ of a possible 15 points

Evaluation of Question # ___
Does the explanation support the answer of true or false?   1   2   3   4   5
Is there good textual evidence to support the answer?   1   2   3   4   5
Is the answer clearly stated?   1   2   3   4   5
                 Total Score _____ of a possible 15 points

Evaluation of Question # ___
Does the explanation support the answer of true or false?   1   2   3   4   5
Is there good textual evidence to support the answer?   1   2   3   4   5
Is the answer clearly stated?   1   2   3   4   5
                 Total Score _____ of a possible 15 points

Copyright 2014

To Kill A Mockingbird Chapters 22-31: Analyzing Passages

Answer the questions following the quotations completely.

1. "'He meant it when he said it,' said Atticus. 'Jem, see if you can stand in Bob Ewell's shoes a minute. I destroyed his last shred of credibility at that trial, if he had any to begin with. The man had to have some kind of comeback, his kind always does. So if spitting in my face and threatening me saved Mayella Ewell one extra beating, that's something I'll gladly take. He had to take it out on somebody and I'd rather it be me than that houseful of children out there. You understand?'"
Do the two separate statements Atticus makes about Bob Ewell fit together logically?

2. "'No, everybody's gotta learn, nobody's born knowin'. That Walter's as smart as he can be, he just gets held back sometimes because he has to stay out and help his daddy. Nothin's wrong with him. Naw, Jem, I think there's just one kind of folks. Folks.'"
What meaning does the repetition of the word "folks" convey?

3. "Aunt Alexandra got up from the table and swiftly passed more refreshments, neatly engaging Mrs. Merriweather and Mrs. Gates in brisk conversation. When she had them well on the road with Mrs. Perkins, Aunt Alexandra stepped back. She gave Miss Maudie a look of pure gratitude, and I wondered at the world of women. Miss Maudie and Aunt Alexandra had never been especially close, and here was Aunty silently thanking her for something. For what, I knew not. I was content to learn that Aunt Alexandra could be pierced sufficiently to feel gratitude for help given. There was no doubt about it, I must soon enter this world, where on its surface fragrant ladies rocked slowly, fanned gently, and drank cool water."
For what does Aunt Alexandra "feel gratitude"?

4. "Mrs. Merriweather faced Mrs. Farrow: 'Gertrude, I tell you there's nothing more distracting than a sulky darky. Their mouths go down to here. Just ruins your day to have one of 'em in the kitchen. You know what I said to my Sophy, Gertrude? I said, 'Sophy,' I said, 'you simply are not being a Christian today. Jesus Christ never went around grumbling and complaining,' and you know, it did her good. She took her eyes off that floor and said, 'Nome, Miz Merriweather, Jesus never went around grumblin'.' I tell you, Gertrude, you never ought to let an opportunity go by to witness for the Lord.'"
How does this passage convey Mrs. Merriweather's ignorance and hypocrisy?

To Kill A Mockingbird Chapters 22-31: Analyzing Passages Page 2

5. "'We had such a good chance,' he said. 'I told him what I thought, but I couldn't in truth say that we had more than a good chance. I guess Tom was tired of white men's chances and preferred to take his own.'"
Why is the repetition of the word "chance" significant?

6. "How could this be so, I wondered, as I read Mr. Underwood's editorial. Senseless killing— Tom had been given due process of law to the day of his death; he had been tried openly and convicted by twelve good men and true; my father had fought for him all the way. Then Mr. Underwood's meaning became clear: Atticus had used every tool available to free men to save Tom Robinson, but in the secret courts of men's hearts Atticus had no case. Tom was a dead man the minute Mayella Ewell opened her mouth and screamed."
Why did "Atticus [have] no case"?

7. "Mr. B. B. Underwood was at his most bitter, and he couldn't have cared less who canceled advertising and subscriptions. (But Maycomb didn't play that way: Mr. Underwood could holler till he sweated and write whatever he wanted to, he'd still get his advertising and subscriptions. If he wanted to make a fool of himself in his paper that was his business.) Mr. Underwood didn't talk about miscarriages of justice, he was writing so children could understand. Mr. Underwood simply figured it was a sin to kill cripples, be they standing, sitting, or escaping. He likened Tom's death to the senseless slaughter of songbirds by hunters and children, and Maycomb thought he was trying to write an editorial poetical enough to be reprinted in The Montgomery Advertiser."
Why is the word "poetical" significant here?

8. "I turned to go home. Street lights winked down the street all the way to town. I had never seen our neighborhood from this angle. There were Miss Maudie's, Miss Stephanie's — there was our house, I could see the porch swing — Miss Rachel's house was beyond us, plainly visible. I could even see Mrs. Dubose's."
Identify words related to seeing. Why are they significant here?

To Kill A Mockingbird Chapters 22-31: Round Characters or Stereotypes

Characterization in literature can be well developed, creating round characters, or developed in a shallow way relying on generalizations, creating stereotype characters. A stereotype is an over generalized belief about a particular group or class of people. An example of a stereotype is that all kids who play sports get low grades or that all students who get high grades are socially awkward. Round characters often have aspects of their personalities which are unexpected in some way. For example, a teacher in a work of fiction who is a "round character" might also be an Olympic athlete. Stereotyped characters conform to generalized expectations. A teacher in a work of fiction who is stereotyped might be mean, unforgiving and strict.

From the list of characters below, put the names of round characters in the relevant boxes and names of stereotype characters in the relevant boxes. Complete the chart, using actual quotes when asked and noting page numbers. Go back and skim the text if you need to, to refresh your memory about these characters.

Scout | Mrs. Merriweather | Miss Maudie | Aunt Alexandra | Atticus | Jem | Dill
Calpurnia | Bob Ewell | Mayella Ewell | Mr. Gilmer | Miss Stephanie

Name of Round Character	Quote – Observation 1 (Find a quote that shows how a character has some unexpected quality.)	Quote – Observation 2 (Find a quote that shows how a character has some unexpected quality.)	How do the unexpected qualities shape your understanding of the character?
Name of Stereotype Character	Quote – Observation 1 (Find a quote that shows how a character has a quality that conforms to a stereotype.)	Quote – Observation 2 (Find a quote that shows how a character has a quality that conforms to a stereotype.)	Does the character conform to a stereotype? Describe the stereotype.

To Kill A Mockingbird Chapters 22-31: Action, Character, Decision

Write **A** (for Action) **C** (for Character) or **D** (for Decision) in the blank next to each to identify whether the passage/statement advances the action, tells us more about a character, or provokes a decision. On the lines under each question, provide a short explanation of your choice.

___ 1. "How could they do it, how could they?"

___ 2. "It was Miss Stephanie's pleasure to tell us: this morning Mr. Bob Ewell stopped Atticus on the post office corner, spat in his face, and told him he'd get him if it took the rest of his life."

___ 3. "'I think I understand,' said Atticus. 'It might be because he knows in his heart that very few people in Maycomb really believed his and Mayella's yarns. He thought he'd be a hero, but all he got for his pain was. . . was, okay, we'll convict this Negro but get back to your dump. He's had his fling with about everybody now, so he ought to be satisfied. He'll settle down when the weather changes.'"

___ 4. "Shuffle-foot had not stopped with us this time. His trousers swished softly and steadily. Then they stopped. He was running, running toward us with no child's steps."

___ 5. "God damn it, I'm not thinking of Jem!"

To Kill A Mockingbird Chapters 22-31: Figurative Language

On the short line provided, write **S** for simile, **M** for metaphor or **I** for idiom. On the lines under each question, explain the meaning and specifically how the figurative language helps create meaning.

___ 1. "It's like bein' a caterpillar in a cocoon, that's what it is," he said. "Like somethin' asleep wrapped up in a warm place. I always thought Maycomb folks were the best folks in the world, least that's what they seemed like."

___ 2. Our father chuckled. "You've many more miles to go, son. A jury's vote's supposed to be secret. Serving on a jury forces a man to make up his mind and declare himself about something. Men don't like to do that. Sometimes it's unpleasant."

___ 3. She took off her glasses and stared at me. "I'll tell you why," she said. "Because — he — is — trash, that's why you can't play with him. I'll not have you around him, picking up his habits and learning Lord-knows-what."

___ 4. "Scout," said Dill, "she just fell down in the dirt. Just fell down in the dirt, like a giant with a big foot just came along and stepped on her. Just ump — " Dill's fat foot hit the ground. "Like you'd step on an ant."

___ 5. Perhaps Atticus was right, but the events of the summer hung over us like smoke in a closed room.

___ 6. "Oh nothing, nothing," she said, "somebody just walked over my grave."

To Kill A Mockingbird Chapters 22-31: Figurative Language Page 2

___ 7. I would show Cecil that we knew he was behind us and we were ready for him. "Cecil Jacobs is a big wet he-en!"

___ 8. Something crushed the chicken wire around me. Metal ripped on metal and I fell to the ground and rolled as far as I could, floundering to escape my wire prison.

___ 9. Someone rolled against me and I felt Jem. He was up like lightning and pulling me with him but, though my head and shoulders were free, I was so entangled we didn't get very far.

___ 10. I ran in the direction of Jem's scream and sank into a flabby male stomach. Its owner said, "Uff!" and tried to catch my arms, but they were tightly pinioned. His stomach was soft but his arms were like steel.

To Kill A Mockingbird Chapters 22-31:
Elements of Fiction & Literary Devices

1. The women's missionary group scene in Chapter 24 is interrupted as Atticus brings news of Tom Robinson's death. What is the dramatic effect of this? Why juxtapose these incidents in this way?

2. Jem asks Scout to put outside a roly-poly bug she finds, rather than kill it. How does this connect with the mockingbird motif?

3. One of the internal conflicts affecting the protagonist Scout is her resistance to acting in a way deemed "feminine" by society. Does a shift occur in these chapters? Why?

4. What effect does the comic element of Scout playing a ham in the Halloween pageant have on the story?

5. How does Harper Lee create suspense that builds to Bob Ewell's attack? How does setting play a role?

6. Scout asks if Jem is dead several times and is told that he is not. Why? Connect your answer to one of the novel's major themes.

To Kill A Mockingbird Chapters 22-31: Meaning & Inferences 1

Read the passages and answer the related questions.

1. *"It's just as much Maycomb County as missionary teas."*

2. *Calpurnia said, "This was all 'round the back steps when I got here this morning. They — they 'preciate what you did, Mr. Finch. They — they aren't oversteppin' themselves, are they?" Atticus's eyes filled with tears. He did not speak for a moment. "Tell them I'm very grateful," he said. "Tell them — tell them they must never do this again. Times are too hard.*

3. *There was a big cake and two little ones on Miss Maudie's kitchen table. There should have been three little ones. It was not like Miss Maudie to forget Dill, and we must have shown it. But we understood when she cut from the big cake and gave the slice to Jem.*

4. *"You couldn't, but they could and did. The older you grow the more of it you'll see. The one place where a man ought to get a square deal is in a courtroom, be he any color of the rainbow, but people have a way of carrying their resentments right into a jury box. As you grow older, you'll see white men cheat black men every day of your life, but let me tell you something and don't you forget it — whenever a white man does that to a black man, no matter who he is, how rich he is, or how fine a family he comes from, that white man is trash."*

5. *She took off her glasses and stared at me. "I'll tell you why," she said. "Because — he — is — trash, that's why you can't play with him. I'll not have you around him, picking up his habits and learning Lord-knows-what. You're enough of a problem to your father as it is."*

6. *"That's what I thought, too," he said at last, "when I was your age. If there's just one kind of folks, why can't they get along with each other? If they're all alike, why do they go out of their way to despise each other? Scout, I think I'm beginning to understand something. I think I'm beginning to understand why Boo Radley's stayed shut up in the house all this time. . . it's because he wants to stay inside."*

To Kill A Mockingbird Chapters 22-31: Meaning & Inferences 2

Read the passage and answer the related questions.

"We're the safest folks in the world," said Miss Maudie. "We're so rarely called on to be Christians, but when we are, we've got men like Atticus to go for us."

Jem grinned ruefully. "Wish the rest of the county thought that."

"You'd be surprised how many of us do."

"Who?" Jem's voice rose. "Who in this town did one thing to help Tom Robinson, just who?"

"His colored friends for one thing, and people like us. People like Judge Taylor. People like Mr. Heck Tate. Stop eating and start thinking, Jem. Did it ever strike you that Judge Taylor naming Atticus to defend that boy was no accident? That Judge Taylor might have had his reasons for naming him?"

This was a thought. Court-appointed defenses were usually given to Maxwell Green, Maycomb's latest addition to the bar, who needed the experience. Maxwell Green should have had Tom Robinson's case.

"You think about that," Miss Maudie was saying. "It was no accident. I was sittin' there on the porch last night, waiting. I waited and waited to see you all come down the sidewalk, and as I waited I thought, Atticus Finch won't win, he can't win, but he's the only man in these parts who can keep a jury out so long in a case like that. And I thought to myself, well, we're making a step — it's just a baby-step, but it's a step."

"'t's all right to talk like that — can't any Christian judges an' lawyers make up for heathen juries," Jem muttered. "Soon's I get grown — "

1. What does "safest" infer? What is the denotation? Connotation?

2. Do Miss Maudie and Jem use the word "Christian" in the same way?

3. Why is the repetition of "waiting" significant?

4. What is the passage conveying about the difference between thought, talk and action?

To Kill A Mockingbird Chapters 22-31:
"What Is The Significance Of Tom Robinson's And Boo Radley's Similarities?"

Though they have radically different lives, Tom Robinson and Boo Radley share many commonalities throughout the novel. As in any work of literature, an author usually takes great care when crafting characters, so these similarities are deliberate and meaningful. Looking closely at the text to uncover this deeper, additional meaning is called *critical reading,* a key skill for accomplished readers.

Using textual evidence from chapters 22-31, look for patterns to begin formulating an answer to the question "What is the significance of these Tom Robinson's and Boo Radley's similarities?". If you consider their appearances, their roles in the community, and their interactions with others in tandem, how do they illuminate major themes in the novel?

To answer these questions:

1. Identify passages and quotes about Tom Robinson's and Boo Radley's appearances, their roles in the community, and their interactions with others.

2. Examine the context of your quotes.

3. Consider the connotation and denotation of key phrases in your quotes.

    a. How are they depicted? Is the information reliable or not? Why?
    b. What conflicts does each character face?
    c. What are the characters revealing or concealing in their language?

4. Look for patterns in your evidence. Is a word or idea repeated? Use these patterns to shape an answer to the question.

To Kill A Mockingbird Chapters 22-31:
"What Is The Significance Of Tom Robinson's And Boo Radley's Similarities?"

Use this chart (and additional pages, if needed) to collect, analyze and evaluate information about Tom Robinson and Boo Radley's shared characteristics.

Quotes from the text	Tom Robinson	Boo Radley	What do they share in common?	Why is the commonality significant?
Quote 1				
Quote 2				
Quote 3				
Quote 4				

To Kill A Mockingbird Chapters 22-31: Creative Analytical Writing Assignments

1. "Translate" the missionary tea conversation, including implied messages. Overall is the conversation positive or negative?

2. Contrast the goal of the missionary society women with how they view people of color in their own communities. Compare their feelings about the Mruna to black people in their own community.

3. Write a stream-of-consciousness paragraph that expresses the thoughts that Mrs. Merriweather's "sulky" maid was thinking as Mrs. Merriweather admonished her about not being Christian.

4. Using facts and quotes from the novel, write Mr. B. B. Underwood's newspaper editorial.

5. Write an essay from Scout's perspective comparing Hitler's treatment of Jewish people to Maycomb's treatment of black people.

6. What is the literal definition of the word "trash"? What does Aunt Alexandra mean when she uses the term "trash"? What does Atticus mean when he uses it? Are their definitions of the term similar? How do their definitions relate to the literal definition?

7. Describe the attack on Jem and Scout from Boo's perspective. How did it catch his attention? When and why did he take action?

8. Does Heck Tate's version of the event allow justice to happen? Why or why not?

9. Is Scout right to be sad about Boo, that "[they] had given him nothing?" Look for evidence in the text.

10. Why does Scout get so emotional when she meets Boo?

To Kill A Mockingbird Chapters 22-31: Quick-Write Writing Assignments

1. Explain Dill's new kind of clown. Does it make sense?
2. Which juror, at first, wanted full acquittal? Why?
3. Why does Aunt Alexandra find Scout socializing with Walter Cunningham distasteful?
4. How is Mrs. Merriweather a hypocrite?
5. What does Scout understand about women after the tea?
6. Was the shooting of Tom Robinson excessive?
7. What does Scout perceive about Miss Gates's opinion of Hitler's treatment of Jewish people?
8. Why does Jem value playing football so much?
9. How is the title Maycomb County Ad Astra Per Aspera apropos?
10. What threatening activities is Bob Ewell doing? What does this show about him?
11. What is Atticus's demeanor when speaking with Heck Tate?
12. What is the story of "The Gray Ghost"? How does it relate to Boo?
13. What is Boo's demeanor like?

MATERIALS: OVERVIEW
TO KILL A MOCKINGBIRD

Reading Activity 1: True or False

Reading Activity 2: Analyzing Passages

Reading Activity 3: Characters' Diction

Reading Activity 4: Action, Character, Decision

Reading Activity 5: Figurative Language

Reading Activity 6: Elements of Fiction & Literary Devices

Reading Activity 7: Meaning and Inferences

Writing Activity 1: Fear In To Kill A Mockingbird

Suggested Writing Assignments

Quick-Write Assignments

NOTES
To Kill A Mockingbird

To Kill a Mockingbird Overview: True or False?

Write *True* or *False* in the blank next to each statement. Below the statement, explain why you chose true or false, referencing the text to support your choices.

_____ 1. Maycomb takes a step forward toward providing fairness for all people regardless of race.

_____ 2. Scout continues to resist behaving in a more ladylike way.

_____ 3. Aunt Alexandra fires Calpurnia.

To Kill a Mockingbird Overview True or False? Page 2

_____ 4. Bob Ewell feels as if he has been humiliated.

_____ 5. Boo Radley kills someone.

_____ 6. Heck Tate will not protect Boo.

To Kill a Mockingbird Overview True or False Evaluation

List Your Group's Members: Your Group's Question # _____

_____   _____   _____

_____   _____   _____

      1 = No, Not At All   **2** = A Little   **3** = Some   **4** = Yes   **5** = Yes, Very Well

Evaluation of Question # ___
Does the explanation support the answer of true or false?   1   2   3   4   5
Is there good textual evidence to support the answer?   1   2   3   4   5
Is the answer clearly stated?   1   2   3   4   5
                      Total Score _____ of a possible 15 points

Evaluation of Question # ___
Does the explanation support the answer of true or false?   1   2   3   4   5
Is there good textual evidence to support the answer?   1   2   3   4   5
Is the answer clearly stated?   1   2   3   4   5
                      Total Score _____ of a possible 15 points

Evaluation of Question # ___
Does the explanation support the answer of true or false?   1   2   3   4   5
Is there good textual evidence to support the answer?   1   2   3   4   5
Is the answer clearly stated?   1   2   3   4   5
                      Total Score _____ of a possible 15 points

Evaluation of Question # ___
Does the explanation support the answer of true or false?   1   2   3   4   5
Is there good textual evidence to support the answer?   1   2   3   4   5
Is the answer clearly stated?   1   2   3   4   5
                      Total Score _____ of a possible 15 points

Evaluation of Question # ___
Does the explanation support the answer of true or false?   1   2   3   4   5
Is there good textual evidence to support the answer?   1   2   3   4   5
Is the answer clearly stated?   1   2   3   4   5
                      Total Score _____ of a possible 15 points

To Kill a Mockingbird Overview Analyzing Passages

Answer the questions following the quotations completely.

1. "You never really understand a person until you consider things from his point of view... until you climb into his skin and walk around in it." Consider the pronouns in this quote.

   Why are they significant?

2. "When a child asks you something, answer him, for goodness' sake. But don't make a production of it. Children are children, but they can spot an evasion quicker than adults, and evasion simply muddles 'em.."

   What does "muddle" mean here? Why is it not optimal?

3. "It was times like these when I thought my father, who hated guns and had never been to any wars, was the bravest man who ever lived."

   What is bravery equated with here?

To Kill a Mockingbird Overview Analyzing Passages Page 2

4. "Atticus, you must be wrong...."

"How's that?"

"Well, most folks seem to think they're right and you're wrong...."

"They're certainly entitled to think that, and they're entitled to full respect for their opinions," said Atticus, "but before I can live with other folks I've got to live with myself. The one thing that doesn't abide by majority rule is a person's conscience."

What does "live with myself" mean here?

5. Family: the world's oldest excuse for telling people what to do. There's no real reason why Atticus's behavior should reflect on anyone but himself and perhaps the parents who raised him, but Aunt Alexandra seems to think it's her business, too. To be fair, given Maycomb's obsession with family, she has a point.

What is the attitude of the narrator?

6. For one thing, Miss Maudie can't serve on a jury because she's a woman-"

"You mean women in Alabama can't-?" I was indignant.

"I do. I guess it's to protect our frail ladies from sordid cases like Tom's. Besides," Atticus grinned, "I doubt if we'd ever get a complete case tried—the ladies'd be interrupting to ask questions."

Jem and I laughed. Miss Maudie on a jury would be impressive. I thought of old Mrs. Dubose in her wheelchair—"Stop that rapping, John Taylor, I want to ask this man something." Perhaps our forefathers were wise.

What can be inferred from the last sentence?

To Kill a Mockingbird Overview Analyzing Passages Page 3

7. I said I would like it very much, which was a lie, but one must lie under certain circumstances and at all times when one can't do anything about them. Scout responds to Atticus's question about Aunt Alexandra coming to live with them.

From the scenarios she explains, infer what a definition of lying might be.

8. Fall, and his children trotted to and fro around the corner, the day's woes and triumphs on their faces. They stopped at an oak tree, delighted, puzzled, apprehensive. Winter, and his children shivered at the front gate, silhouetted against a blazing house. Winter, and a man walked into the street, dropped his glasses, and shot a dog. Summer, and he watched his children's heart break. Autumn again, and Boo's children needed him.

What is the effect of the possessive pronouns here?

To Kill a Mockingbird Overview: Characters' Diction

Characterization is the method by which an author creates a character. Characterization occurs through direct descriptions of characters and indirectly by the way the characters behave and speak. Characters often have certain patterns of speech associated with them and specific levels of diction, or verbal levels of correctness, clearness, or effectiveness.

Complete the chart, using actual quotes when asked and noting page numbers. Go back and skim the text if you need to, to refresh your memory about these characters.

Quote	Who Said It?	What words or grammatical patterns stand out?	What does this show about the character?
"Miss Jean Louise, stand up. Your father's passin'."			
As you grow older, you'll see white men cheat black men every day of your life, but let me tell you something and don't you forget it -- whenever a white man does that to a black man, no matter who he is, how rich he is, or how fine a family he comes from, that white man is trash.			
Folks don't like to have somebody around knowing more than they do. It aggravates them. You're not going to change any of them by talking right, they've got to want to learn themselves, and when they don't want to learn there's nothing you can do but keep your mouth shut or talk their language			
"well, it'd be sort of like shootin' a mockingbird, wouldn't it?"			
"He took advantage of me. An' if you fine, fancy gentlemen ain't gonna do nothin' about it, then you're just a bunch of lousy, yella, stinkin' cowards...'			

To Kill a Mockingbird Overview: Action, Character, Decision

Select one of the characters listed below. For that character, identify three passages from the novel, answering the questions below.

Characters: Scout, Jem, Atticus, Aunt Alexandra, Miss Maudie, Calpurnia

1. Find a passage in the text that reveals more about who this character is.

    Page number _____

    Copy or summarize your selected quote.

    Explain how the passage reveals more about the character, identifying specific words or phrases from your passage.

2. Find a passage in the text that reveals how this character made a decision.
    Page number _____

    Copy or summarize your selected quote.

    Explain how the passage reveals how the character is provoked to make a decision, identifying specific words or phrases from your passage.

To Kill a Mockingbird Overview Action, Character, Decision Page 2

3. Find a passage in the text that reveals how this character took action.

   Page number _____

   Copy or summarize your selected quote.

   Explain how the passage reveals how the character is prompted to take action, identifying specific words or phrases from your passage.

To Kill a Mockingbird Overview: Figurative Language

On the short line provided, write P for personification, S for simile, H for hyperbole, I for idiom, or M for metaphor. In the space under each question, explain what the figurative language means.

_____ 1. Less than two weeks later we found a whole package of chewing gum, which we enjoyed; the fact that everything on the Radley Place was poison having slipped Jem's memory.

_____ 2. Ladies bathed before noon, after their three-o'clock naps, and by nightfall were like soft teacakes with frostings of sweat and sweet talcum.

_____ 3. From the day Mr. Radley took Arthur home, people say the house died.

_____ 4. She looked and smelled like a peppermint drop.

_____ 5. The remains of a picket drunkenly guarded the front yard.

_____ 6. ...but then Uncle Jack was strange. He said he was trying to get Miss Maudie's goat, that he had been trying unsuccessfully for forty years....

To Kill a Mockingbird Overview: Figurative Language Page 2

_____ 7. "The world's endin', Atticus! Please do something-!" I dragged him to the window and pointed.

_____ 8. The Radley place fascinated Dill. In spite of our warnings it drew him as the moon draws water…

_____ 9. The misery of the house began many years before Jem and I were born.

_____ 10. Well how'd you feel if you'd been shut up for a hundred years with nothin' but cats to eat? I bet he's got a beard down to here.

To Kill a Mockingbird Overview: Elements of Fiction & Literary Devices

When he was nearly thirteen, my brother Jem got his arm badly broken at the elbow. When it healed, and Jem's fears of never being able to play football were assuaged, he was seldom self-conscious about his injury. His left arm was somewhat shorter than his right; when he stood or walked, the back of his hand was at right angles to his body, his thumb parallel to his thigh. He couldn't have cared less, so long as he could pass and punt.

When enough years had gone by to enable us to look back on them, we sometimes discussed the events leading to his accident. I maintain that the Ewells started it all, but Jem, who was four years my senior, said it started long before that. He said it began the summer Dill came to us, when Dill first gave us the idea of making Boo Radley come out.

I said if he wanted to take a broad view of the thing, it really began with Andrew Jackson. If General Jackson hadn't run the Creeks up the creek, Simon Finch would never have paddled up the Alabama, and where would we be if he hadn't?

We were far too old to settle an argument with a fist-fight, so we consulted Atticus. Our father said we were both right.

1. These are the first paragraphs of the novel, yet the ending is revealed. Why is this significant?

2. The novel is told from the first person retrospective perspective. How does this create nostalgia and/or a sense of personal history?

3. How does the perspective of this novel invite a longer view of history? Why does the narrator mention Andrew Jackson?

4. Why is it significant that the narrator suggests the historical perspective? What can be inferred about her from this? What can be inferred from Jem's belief that the events began with Boo Radley?

5. Why it is significant that Atticus says that both are right? How might this influence the way a reader interprets the novel?

To Kill a Mockingbird Overview: Meaning & Inferences 1

Read the passages and answer the related questions.

1. You are too young to understand it ... but sometimes the Bible in the hand of one man is worse than a whiskey bottle in the hand of--oh, of your father.

What is the point of Miss Maudie's comparison? How can the Bible be misused?

2. Neighbors bring food with death and flowers with sickness and little things in between. Boo was our neighbor. He gave us two soap dolls, a broken watch and chain, a pair of good-luck pennies, and our lives. But neighbors give in return. We never put back into the tree what we took out of it: we had given him nothing, and it made me sad.

Is Scout's statement that they gave Boo Radley "nothing" accurate?

3. "…all I can say is, when you and Jem are grown, maybe you'll look back on this with some compassion and some feeling that I didn't let you down."

What does Atticus mean by "let you down"?

4. Atticus had promised me he would wear me out if he ever heard of me fighting anymore; I was far too old and too big for such childish things, and the sooner I learned to hold in, the better off everybody would be.

Why is this ironic?

5. Boo saw me run instinctively to the bed where Jem was sleeping, for the same shy smile crept across his face. Hot with embarrassment, I tried to cover up by covering Jem up.

Why a "shy smile"?

To Kill a Mockingbird Overview: Meaning & Inferences 2

Read the passage and answer the related questions.

"Very good, Cecil," said Miss Gates. Puffing, Cecil returned to his seat. A hand went up in the back of the room. "How can he do that?"

"Who do what?" asked Miss Gates patiently.

"I mean how can Hitler just put a lot of folks in a pen like that, looks like the govamint'd stop him," said the owner of the hand.

"Hitler is the government," said Miss Gates, and seizing an opportunity to make education dynamic, she went to the blackboard. She printed DEMOCRACY in large letters. "Democracy," she said. "Does anybody have a definition?"

"Us," somebody said.

I raised my hand, remembering an old campaign slogan Atticus had once told me about.

"What do you think it means, Jean Louise?"

"'Equal rights for all, special privileges for none'," I quoted.

"Very good, Jean Louise, very good," Miss Gates smiled. In front of DEMOCRACY, she printed WE ARE A. "Now class, say it all together, 'We are a democracy'."

We said it. Then Miss Gates said, "That's the difference between America and Germany. We are a democracy and Germany is a dictatorship.

"Dictator-ship," she said. "Over here we don't believe in persecuting anybody. Persecution comes from people who are prejudiced. Pre-judice," she enunciated carefully. "There are no better people in the world than the Jews, and why Hitler doesn't think so is a mystery to me."

An inquiring soul in the middle of the room said, "Why don't they like the Jews, you reckon, Miss Gates?"

"I don't know, Henry. They contribute to every society they live in, and most of all, they are a deeply religious people. Hitler's trying to do away with religion, so maybe he doesn't like them for that reason."

1. What is significant about the use of the word "folks" here? How does it connect to other points in the novel?

2. What is the tone of the phrase "seizing an opportunity to make education dynamic"?

To Kill a Mockingbird Overview: Meaning & Inferences 2 Page 2

3. Why the repetition of "we are a democracy"? Why is it significant?

4. What does Miss Gates say about Jewish people?

5. Why is this whole scene ironic?

To Kill a Mockingbird: *What Role Does Fear Play In To Kill A Mockingbird?*

The first chapter of the novel alludes to a very famous line from FDR's First Inaugural Address:

> …People moved slowly then. They ambled across the square, shuffled in and out of the stores around it, took their time about everything. A day was twenty-four hours long but seemed longer. There was no hurry, for there was nowhere to go, nothing to buy and no money to buy it with, nothing to see outside the boundaries of Maycomb County. But it was a time of vague optimism for some of the people: Maycomb County had recently been told that <u>it had nothing to fear but fear itself</u>.

Fear, in different iterations, plays an important role in *To Kill A Mockingbird* as a major theme. In an essay, explore the truth of the quote by answering the question "What role does fear play in *To Kill A Mockingbird?*"

Fear manifests itself in a variety of ways in the text and is made evident by multiple relationships between different characters. Select one way that you see fear presented in the novel and focus on it. Identify a selection of related quotes and annotate them. Examine how characters interact with one another and what significance their actions have. Looking closely at the text for this deeper, additional meaning is called *critical reading,* a key skill for accomplished readers.

Using textual evidence you have gathered, look for patterns to begin formulating an answer to the question "What role does fear play in *To Kill A Mockingbird?*". As you develop an answer, consider how you can restate your discovery as a thesis.

To determine a thesis about the significance of fear in the novel:

1. Identify passages and quotes focused on one way you see fear manifested in the novel

2. Examine the context of your quotes.

3. Consider the connotation and denotation of key phrases in your quotes. Annotate them thoroughly.

    a. Does a character manifestly express fear? Or is it latent?
    b. Is the basis for the fear sound? Does the character fear a real danger, or is the character "fearing fear?"
    c. What are the characters revealing or concealing in their language? Is their fear evident?

4. Look for patterns in your evidence. Is a word or idea repeated? Use these patterns to shape an answer to the question and to formulate a thesis.

What Role Does Fear Play In To Kill A Mockingbird?

Use this chart (and additional pages, if needed) to collect, analyze and evaluate information about fear in *To Kill A Mockingbird*.

Quote and page number	Paraphrase main idea	What is causing the fear?	Any interesting words or phrases?	How does this relate to fear as a conceptual idea? ("So what?")

What observations, patterns or discoveries have you made? "So what" about fear?

To Kill a Mockingbird: "What role does fear play in *To Kill A Mockingbird?*" Page 3

Whenever you are writing, it is critical that you have a point, whether it is your intention to persuade, inform, entertain or instruct.

Let's make sure your essay about fear has a point. *So What?* is the magic question to ask yourself whenever you are reaching beyond observation toward a thesis.

<u>Complete the questions below</u>:

What observation of your primary source do you think is most important?

(Example: Jem is afraid of the Radley House, even though he lies and says he is not.)

Taking your answer to the previous question, consider this: So what? Figure out why your discovery is meaningful. Push yourself to think about conceptual ideas and deeper thematic issues.

Now, take the discovery you've made about the significance of your topic and craft a test thesis. My test thesis is:

To Kill a Mockingbird Overview: Creative Analytical Writing Assignments

1. Having completed reading the whole novel, what is the significance of the gifts Boo gave the children?

2. How is poverty a factor in many of the conflicts that occur in the novel?

3. As a reader, which character do you wish was more developed and that the text revealed more about him or her? Explain why.

4. Education plays a significant role in the novel, especially as it shapes Scout. What is the novel suggesting about the importance of education to children? What is its highest goal?

5. Do characters show a responsibility for being good citizens of Maycomb? Select a few characters and provide examples, explaining how their actions serve the greater good of the community.

6. Considering the Gothic elements, can this novel be described as a thriller or a mystery? Cite examples from the text.

7. Which characters in the novel are oppressed or treated differently? What allows this treatment to occur?

8. At multiple points in the novel, Atticus, Jem or Scout mention possible future careers in law for the children. Find relevant quotes and consider them. How has the experience with the trial (and its after effects) prepared Jem and Scout for careers in law?

9. How does the novel define courage (consider Atticus explaining it to Jem as they discussed Mrs. Dubose)? With that definition in mind, what is the most courageous act that a character in the novel makes?

10. Imagine that sexism, not racism, was central to the book. Imagine that the focus of the trial was on how Mayella is a victim. How would that shift change your understanding of major themes like justice or morality?

To Kill a Mockingbird Overview: Quick-Write Writing Assignments

1. Why is the title of the novel meaningful?

2. Which characters are "mockingbirds"?

3. Which characters are the most or least moral? Why?

4. Have the children's imaginings of Boo Radley come true in some version? Explain.

5. What gifts do characters in the novel give or receive?

6. Does Scout become a "lady?"

7. Describe Atticus's parenting style. How is it a benefit to his children?

8. Several minor characters like Mr. Avery and Miss Stephanie provide a backdrop for understanding the main characters and their actions. Which minor characters best embody the values of Maycomb?

9. Why are all the animals in the novel: turtle, rabid dog, mockingbird, blue jay, roly-poly bug? What is there to learn from this motif?

10. Does following the law lead to justice in this novel? Consider multiple examples.

www.ingramcontent.com/pod-product-compliance
Lightning Source LLC
Chambersburg PA
CBHW081450070526
44586CB00019B/2287